NATURE STUDY IN ELEMENTARY SCHOOLS, FIRST READER

Published @ 2017 Trieste Publishing Pty Ltd

ISBN 9780649655588

Nature Study in Elementary Schools, First Reader by Lucy Langdon Williams Wilson

Edited by Trieste Publishing Pty Ltd.
 Cover @ 2017

www.triestepublishing.com

LUCY LANGDON WILLIAMS WILSON

NATURE STUDY IN ELEMENTARY SCHOOLS, FIRST READER

 Trieste

LUCY LANGDON WILLIAMS WILSON

NATURE STUDY IN
ELEMENTARY
SCHOOLS, FIRST READER

Trieste

Frontispiece

NATURE STUDY

IN

ELEMENTARY SCHOOLS

FIRST READER

BY

LUCY LANGDON WILLIAMS WILSON, Ph.D.

OF THE PHILADELPHIA NORMAL SCHOOL

AUTHOR OF "NATURE STUDY IN ELEMENTARY SCHOOLS: A MANUAL," "NATURE
STUDY IN ELEMENTARY SCHOOLS: A READER," "HISTORY IN
ELEMENTARY SCHOOLS: A MANUAL," AND "HISTORY
IN ELEMENTARY SCHOOLS: A READER"

New York
THE MACMILLAN COMPANY
LONDON: MACMILLAN & CO., Ltd.
1901

Norwood Press
J. S. Cushing & Co. — Berwick & Smith
Norwood Mass. U.S.A.

PREFACE

THE original matter in this series of Readers has
been written, and the selections chosen, with the
desire of putting into the hands of little children
literature which shall have for their minds the same
interest and value that really good books and maga-
zines have for grown-up people. It is the author's
aim to prepare the ground and even thus early to
plant the seeds of that which may later develop into
a love for art, for literature, and for nature.

But this most desirable result cannot be accom-
plished by merely putting the Readers into the hands
of the child, expecting him to master the words by
reading the sentences, — to get at the thought
while he stumbles and hesitates over unfamiliar
words.

It is expected that each of these lessons will be
preceded by a nature lesson.

For a guide in this work, both for facts and
method, I know of nothing better than my own
book, "Nature Study: A Manual for Teachers."
These Readers have been planned in accordance with
the course of study there outlined.

Either during the nature lesson or after it, the
new words should be thoroughly taught from the

v

board.   To aid the teacher a list of such words has
been placed at the beginning of each lesson.

Later in the day let him read the reading lesson
for the sake of the thought.   Do not take it for
granted that no further teaching is necessary.   But
remember, too, that it is now the pupil's time to
talk.

If he does not read well now, it is because he
fails to grasp the thought.   A word, a question, will
often clear up the obscurity in his mind.   Lead him
to think, not to imitate.

It is a good idea to have a systematic plan for
silent reading.   Many of the stories in this volume
will lend themselves easily to this device.   And on
this work may be based a subsequent oral and written language lesson.

Above all, do not neglect to cultivate his taste —
his literary and artistic instincts.   *" What stanza,
what line, or what part of this did you like the best?"*
" Why?" are questions always in order and always
interesting.

Two devices, well known but comparatively little
employed, are most useful in developing a child's
literary and artistic nature ; viz. the learning of
poetry, and the listening to reading aloud.   For this
purpose the lists of literature in the Manual will be
found very useful.

L. L. W. WILSON.

PHILADELPHIA NORMAL SCHOOL,
    September, 1898.

TABLE OF CONTENTS

[1] By permission of Messrs. Houghton, Mifflin & Co.
[2] By permission of Messrs. Little, Brown & Co.

OCTOBER

NOVEMBER

[1] By permission of *The Youth's Companion*.
[2] By permission of Miss Emilie Poulsson.
[3] By permission of Messrs. Routledge & Co.

DECEMBER

JANUARY

[1] By permission of Messrs. Houghton, Mifflin & Co.
[2] By permission of *The Youth's Companion*.
[3] By permission of Messrs. The Oliver Ditson Company.
[4] By permission of Miss Emilie Poulsson.

    [1] By permission of Messrs. Houghton, Mifflin & Co.
    [2] By permission of *The Youth's Companion.*

[1] By permission of Messrs. Copeland & Day.
[2] By permission of Messrs. The Educational Publishing Co., Boston.
[3] By permission of Messrs. Ginn & Company.
[4] By permission of Messrs. The Oliver Ditson Company.

JUNE

[1] By permission of Messrs. Copeland & Day.
[2] By permission of Messrs. Houghton, Mifflin & Co.
[3] By permission of Mr. Morgan Bates.

SEPTEMBER

THE CLOUDS

clouds   moving   voice   shepherd

I like to look up into the sky.
It is so blue and far away.
Even the soft white clouds are far away.
See! They are moving across the sky.
They look like white, white sheep.
Listen! Do you hear the voice of the shep-
herd boy?

$$oo — oo — oo — oo !$$
$$m — m — m — m !$$

Look! the clouds are moving faster.
Shepherd Wind is driving them home.
Good-by, dear clouds, good-by.

*   *   *   *   *   *   *

White sheep, white sheep,
On a blue hill,
Do you eat forget-me-nots
When you stand so still?

3

driven   perhaps   sometimes   field   army

Where are all the pretty sheep to-day ?
Shepherd Wind must have driven them away.
The sky is as blue as forget-me-nots.
I wish that I were a kite.
Perhaps Shepherd Wind would carry me up
into the sky.

* * * * * * *

Sometimes the sky is dark gray.
Then we cannot see the sun.
The dark rain clouds hide him from us.
Then rain begins to fall.

See, it walks across the fields.
It moves like a great army.

THE RAIN

lifted   need   rubber   umbrella   scampered

Who likes the rain?
" I," said the grass.
" I," said all the little flowers.
" I," said the brook.
And " I," said a little boy.
Then the rain began to fall.
The flowers lifted up their pretty heads.
" Thank you," they said to the kind rain.
The brook was glad too.
" I need every drop," he said.
" For I want to be a great big river."
The little boy said : —
" The rain does so much good.
" And it does not hurt me.
" For I have rubber boots.
" I have a rain coat, and an umbrella.
" And this is what I call fun."
And off he scampered to school.

THE WIND

shakes rattles autumn somewhere

Shepherd Wind has great fun these days.

He blows the seeds away.

He makes the leaves fall.

He shakes the apples from the trees.

He takes the hats right off the heads of little children.

He turns umbrellas inside out.

He blows dust into our eyes.

He rattles the windows and doors.

At night he is tired.

He stops his play.

I wonder where he sleeps.

* * * * *

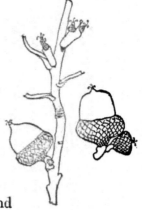

"In Autumn,
   When the wind is up,
I know the acorn's
   Out his cup,

   For 'tis the wind
      Who takes it out,
   And plants an oak
      Somewhere about."

—F. D. SHERMAN.

THE THISTLE

dining room   beautiful   fragrant   dinner

What is this?

This is the thistle.

But the bees think that it is their dining room.

And is it not a beautiful dining room?

How fragrant it is!

What does the thistle give the bees for dinner?

The thistle likes to have the bees visit her.

They put her flower dust just where she wants it.

That is why she is so red and so fragrant.

She says to the bees: —

"I am beautiful, that you may see me.

"I am fragrant, that you may find me.

"Come to me.

"I will give you something good to eat."

*   *   *   *   *   *   *

touches   punishment   cattle   reason

Here is the thistle again!

These are her leaves.

Do they say : —

"Come to me, for I am beautiful"?

No, they say : —

"No one touches me without punishment."

To whom do the leaves say this?

They say it to the cattle.

Perhaps this is the reason that thistles grow where nothing else will.

What do you think about it?

*   *   *   *   *   *   *

donkey   balloons   basket   traveller

And here is the thistle again !
The bees are not near her flowers now.
Even the donkey will not eat her dry leaves.
But look at the little balloons !

See how they fly in the wind.
The top part is of finest silk.
Below is a little basket.

In this basket lies a little traveller asleep.

The wind will carry him far from his mother.

But this will not hurt him.

He will not even know about it.

He will sleep away until spring.

Then he will creep out of his basket.
He will work and work and work.
And he will grow and grow and grow.
And at last he will be a beautiful thistle just like his mother.

*   *   *   *   *   *   *

learned   golden rod
robin   called
of course

Once
there was
a little girl.
She loved to go
to the woods.
She said often : —

"Oh! see that pretty flower. Oh! look at that beautiful bird."

But as she grew older she learned to say : —

"Oh! there is the golden rod! Oh! look at the robin."

And the flowers and the birds liked to hear their names.

Do you like to be called just " little girl " ?

Or do you like to be called just " little boy " ?

No; you like to be called by your right name, of course.

And do you know the names of the flowers?

I will help you to learn them.

SEPTEMBER'S FLOWERS

branches   torches   butterflies   cousin
aster

This is the golden rod.

Look at its branches.

Do they not remind you of the elm tree ?

But their heads are yellow, not green.

They look like torches along the road,

City people would not say torches.

They would say street lamps. Sometimes the butterflies and bees are late coming home.

The golden rod lamps help them to find the way.

And here is a cousin of the golden rod.

It is the aster, or star flower.

———◆———

OTHER COUSINS OF THE GOLDEN ROD

Black-eyed-Susan   Chicory
waken   risen

The golden rod and aster have many cousins.

One of them is called the sun flower. She was named for the sun because she loves it.

She watches the sun all day long.
When the sun moves, she moves.
Do you like to look at things that you love?

My name is Black-
eyed-Susan.

And mine is Chicory.
My eyes are blue.
But like my cousin, I love the sun.
When he sleeps, I shut my eyes too.
I do not waken until the sun has risen.

SOME OF THE GOLDEN ROD'S FRIENDS

**relatives   different   nasturtium   insects
hidden   spur**

We are not relatives of the golden rod.
But we are their friends.
We open our flowers in the autumn too.
But some of us live in very different places.

My name is the garden nasturtium.
The insects visit me, for I have a great deal
of honey.
It is hidden in this long spur.
Taste it.   Is it not good?

carrot   everybody   vase   lace
morning glories   Jamestown weed

I am the wild carrot.

Every one knows me.

But not everybody knows my name.

Very few people know how beautiful I am.

Put me by myself in a vase.

Do I not look like lace?

Some people call me Bird's Nest.

Can you see the reason why?

* * *   * * * *

I grow by the roadside too.

And I am much more beautiful than people think.

My flowers look like morning glories.

But I am not a morning glory.

I grow on a bush, not on a vine.

My name is Jamestown weed.

THE BEES

sucks   mouth   real   stomach   basket
market

What does the bee do with the honey?
What does he make with flower dust?
The honey he sucks up into his mouth.
But it does not go to his real stomach.
He keeps it in a nice little bag.
For he does not want it all for himself.
He gets it for his little sisters and brothers,
or he puts it away for winter.
The flower dust he carries home in a basket.
Where does your mother carry her market
basket?
The bee carries his on his leg.
It is always ready for use.

c

TO A HONEY BEE

Busy body, busy body,
Always on the wing;
   Wait a bit
      Where you have lit,
      And tell me what
        you sing.

Up and in the air again,
Flap, flap, flap!
  And now she stops,
  And now she drops,
Into the rose's lap.

Come just a minute, come,
From your rose so red;
  Hum, hum,
  Hum, hum, —
That was all she said.

Busy body, busy body,
Always light and gay;
It seems to me,
For all I see,
Your work is only play.

— ALICE CARY.

another   worker   caterpillar
damage foolish helping

And here is another hard worker.

His name is the caterpillar.

But he does a great deal of damage. He eats the leaves from the trees.

We do not want our trees eaten up.

Shall we kill the caterpillars then?

Birds eat caterpillars. We do not want to take away the birds' dinner.

No; for we love the birds.

But why are there so many caterpillars?

Why do not the birds eat them up?

Perhaps some one has killed the birds?

Surely no one would be so foolish.

Perhaps not.

But sometimes boys take birds' eggs from the nest.

And birds' eggs become birds.

Let us kill caterpillars by helping the birds.

———◆———

THE GRASSHOPPER FAMILY

grasshopper   rubbing   Katy did
better   clothes

How do you do, Mr. Grasshopper?

What a long pair of legs you have!

Perhaps that is why you can jump so far.

But I have seen you fly too.

Look! Look! He is singing, but not with his mouth.

He is rubbing his legs against his wings.

What does he say?

He says, —

" Zip — zip — zip — ze-e-e-e-e.

" This is my cousin, Miss Katy did.

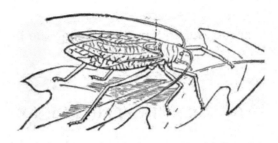

" She can talk much better than I.

"She is more beautiful.

" Her dress is of green.

" But then she lives in the trees.

" My dress is the color of the dry grass where I live.

" We each of us have just the clothes that we need."

THE CONCERT

odors　　fireflies　　darkness　　thousand
crickets　　screeched

All day long grasshoppers had sung their
song : —
Zip — zip — zip — ze-e-e-e-e.
And the bees had told their story : —
Hum — hum — hum.
But now it was dusk.
Grasshoppers and bees had gone to bed.
The flowers sent out their sweetest odors.
The fireflies lit up the darkness.
And then the real concert began.
" Katy did — did — did.
" Katy didn't — didn't — did — did — did."
" Tr-r-r-r-r-rdt," went the tree toad.
A thousand crickets joined in the chorus.
"Chirp! Chirp!! Chirp!!!"
The frogs croaked.
The screech owl screeched.

　　　*　　*　　*　　*　　*　　*　　*

We know that this happens every night.
But would you believe it ?
Some people have never heard it.

SEPTEMBER

**orchards   bending   tokens
summer   autumn**

The golden rod is yellow;
The corn is turning brown;
The trees in apple orchards
With fruit are bending down.

* ;* * * *

By all these lovely tokens
September days are here,
With summer's best of weather
And autumn's best of cheer.

—HELEN HUNT JACKSON.

OCTOBER

"October's bright blue weather!"

A BIT OF ADVICE

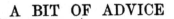

Lady bug, Lady
bug,
If I were you,
I would always carry
A bucket of dew,
To dash on my house, if it burned,
And then, may be,
I'd save every little Lady bug baby.

— *Youth's Companion.*

AN OAK GALL

Here is another queer little house.

It grows on the oak.

But it is not an acorn.

It has no door nor any windows.

But some day a little insect will come out of it.

How did he get in?

I will tell you.

Here is Mother Gall Fly.

One day she made a hole in the oak twig.

She cut it with her sword.

Inside the hole she put an egg. In a short time this little house grew around the egg. The oak built the house.

Perhaps she wanted to get the egg as far from her as she could.

whisper   weather vane
least   whichever   heart

Where did Shepherd Wind come from to-day?

How do you know?

Did the leaves whisper it to you?

Or did the weather vane tell you?

Here is the weather vane.

N stands for North.
E stands for East.
S stands for South.
W stands for West.

" Wind from the north or east
　　You I like least,
　　Wind from the south and west
　　You I like best."

What kind of weather does Shepherd Wind
bring with him from the east?
Let us watch and find out.

" Whichever way the wind doth blow,
　　Some heart is glad to have it so.
　　Then blow it east or blow it west,
　　The wind that blows, that wind is best."

milkweed   dandelion   whisked   journey
companion   ailanthus

The milkweed spoke: —

"You are not the only plant who makes balloons for her seed babies.

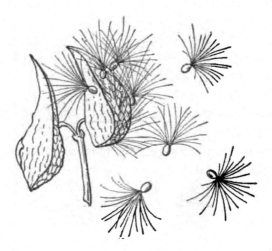

"Look at me."

"And look at me too," said the dandelion.

Just then Shepherd Wind came along.

Quicker than a wink, he whisked away the babies.

What a long journey they took!

Here are some of their companions.

This is the Maple Seed, with its two wings.

And Mr. Ash.

And Mr. Ailanthus, with only one wing.

At last the babies landed on the ground.

Here they saw other babies without their mothers.

Shepherd Wind did not bring them.

What did, I wonder?

Perhaps a little boy.

Or a sheep!

THE CHESTNUT BURR

**chestnut   burr   spines   painted
knocked   opened**

Look at this little green house.

All summer long three children have been growing, growing, growing.

I think that it has been a safe little house.

For look at its sharp spines.

They say: —

" Do not touch us.

" It will not be safe to do so."

Here is the little house again.

It is no longer green.

The Wind has painted it brown.

He whistled so loud at his work that the babies began to waken.

Then Jack Frost came and knocked at the door.

"Come out, little children, come play with me."

But Jack Frost had to knock many times before the door opened.

different   velvet   tired   shiny   enjoy frolic

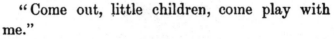

Here is the little house again.

And here are the three little chestnut children.

Do you think that they are all alike?

No, indeed. They are as different as other brothers and sisters.

D

What a beautiful house.

It is as soft as velvet inside.

But the children are tired of their lovely home.

They want to go out into the world.

When Jack Frost opens the door,

They will go out with Shepherd Wind.

What a life he will lead them!

But their shiny coats will keep them dry.

And so they will enjoy the frolic.

But at last they will be tired out.

Then they will go to sleep till spring comes to waken them.

THE WIND AND THE SUN

"I blow," said the wind.
  "Then I bow," said the tree,
"And I fly," said the cloud,
  "Then I frown," said the sea.

"I shine," said the sun.
  "Then I bloom," said the tree
"And I float," said the cloud
  "Then I smile," said the sea.

— From Youth's Companion.

THE SUN

sunbeams soldiers forward arrows
bravely conquer

The sunbeams are the soldiers of the sun.
Every morning they march forward.
They cross deep seas and rivers.
They climb high mountains.
They shoot their shining arrows.

Who is it that they fight so bravely?
It is the night.
Every morning they conquer the night.
But every evening she returns again.
Still the sun really conquers even then.
For the moonlight is sunlight.
The sun shines on the moon.
And the moon sends it back to us.

THE SUN AGAIN

Did you know that the sun is always shining?
It shines even at night.
But our world is always turning around.
So at night it takes us away from the sun.
The sun is working in China while we sleep here.
And when the people of China sleep, the sun works for us.
What does the sun do?
He gives us the light.
He helps the plants to grow.
He warms us.
He carries water up into the sky.
He gives us the beautiful rainbow!
And at the foot of the rainbow lies a pot of gold.

GOOD MORNING, MERRY SUNSHINE

morning   sunshine   scared   stopped
    staying   staid

Good morning, merry sunshine,
    How did you wake so soon?
You have scared the little stars away,
    And driven away the moon.

I saw you go to sleep last night,
    Before I stopped my playing;
How did you get 'way over there,
    And where have you been staying?

I never go to sleep, dear child,
    I just go 'round to see
My little children of the east,
    Who rise and watch for me.

I waken all the birds and bees
    And flowers on my way,
And last of all the little child
    Who staid out late to play.

— EMILIE POULSSON.

SUNSHINE STORIES

pardon   howling   silence

"I am going to tell a story," said the Wind.

"I beg your pardon," said the Rain.

" It is my turn now.

" You have been howling long enough."

" I will speak myself," said the Sunshine.

" Silence, both of you."

The Wind stopped talking at once.

Then the Rain beat against him.

He shook him, and said : —

" We won't stand it.

"She is always breaking through — is Madame Sunshine.

" What she has to say is not worth hearing."

Still the Sunshine began to talk.

This is what she said : —

THE FIRST STORY

waves   feathers   fortune   merchant   ship

A swan flew over the waves of the ocean.

It was a bird of Good Fortune.

Every one of its feathers shone like gold.

One of them drifted to a great merchant ship.
It fell on the curly hair of a young man.

It touched his forehead.
It became a pen in his hand.
It brought him luck.
Soon he became a wealthy merchant.

THE SECOND STORY

farther   shade   wonderful   pillow

The swan flew farther and farther away.
At last he came to a sunny, green meadow.
There was in this meadow only one tree.
Under its shade a little boy lay asleep.
The swan kissed one of the leaves of the tree.
It fell into the boy's hand.

And as it fell, it changed into three leaves —
to ten — to a whole book.

In this wonderful book he read about the
birds.

It told him of the flowers and the trees.

He read in it about the stones, and everything
good.

At night he laid the book under his pillow.

He did not want to forget what he had been
reading.

This wonderful book led him to a school.

And from the school he went everywhere.

He was studying all the time.

"I have seen his name among the names
of wise men," said the Sunshine.

THE THIRD STORY

reeds   pecking   cracked   opened

The swan flew into the quiet woods.

He rested awhile on a deep, dark lake.

A poor woman was gathering dry sticks for
fire wood.

In her arms she held her little child.

She saw the golden swan, as he rose from
the reeds.

What was it that shone so?

A golden egg that was still quite warm.

She put it next her heart.

Soon she heard a gentle pecking inside the shell.

But she thought it was the beating of her own heart.

In her little house, she took out the egg.

"Tick! tick!" it said as if it had been a golden watch.

But it was not.

It was an egg — a real, living egg.

The egg cracked and opened.

Out came a dear little baby swan.

Around its neck were four rings.

The woman had four boys.

So she knew at once, that there was one ring for each boy.

Just as she took them the bird flew away.

She kissed each of the rings.

She made each of the children kiss one.

She laid it over his heart.

Then she put it on his finger.

"I saw it all," said the Sunshine.

"And I saw what happened afterward."

* * * * * * *

turned   Jason   Golden Fleece
squeezed   musician   poet

One of the boys was playing beside a brook.
He picked up a lump of clay.

He turned and twisted it.

At last it looked like Jason who found the Golden Fleece.

The second boy ran into the meadow.

He gathered a handful of beautiful flowers.

He squeezed them tightly.

The juice flew into his eyes and on his hands.

After many a day, and many a year, he became a great painter.

The third child held the ring in his teeth.
It made a beautiful sound.
It was only the echo of a song in his heart.
But it was the beginning.
He became at last a great musician

And the fourth little one — yes, he was the " ugly duck " of the family.

" But I gave him warm sunny kisses," said the Sunshine.

"And he became a great poet."

* * * * * * *

stupid tiresome fisherman amber

"That was a very long story," said the Wind.

" And so stupid and tiresome," said the Rain.

" Blow on me, Wind, that I may feel better."

While the Wind blew, the Sunshine said : —

The swan of fortune flew over a lovely bay.

Here some fishermen were setting their nets.

To the poorest of them the swan gave a piece of amber.

Amber draws things toward itself.

And it drew hearts to his poor little house.

The fisherman and his wife were happy in their little home.

And so their life became a real sunshine story.

* * * * * * *

"I think that we had better stop now," said the Wind.

"I am very tired.

"And I am sure that the Sunshine has talked long enough."

"I think so too," said the Rain.

And what do we say?

We say, "Now the story is done."

— Adapted from ANDERSEN.

THE FALLING LEAVES

**branches   cared   plenty   clothes
dresses**

The leaves have been hard at work.

Look at the ends of the branches. See what they have made.

These baby buds have been well cared for.

The leaves have given them plenty of warm, dry clothes.

* * * * * * *

Shepherd Wind has been talking to the leaves.

He has been saying: —

"Come, put on your bright dresses.

"Then we will have a fine frolic.

"And then there will be more good work for you."

So the leaves put on their gowns of yellow and red.

They flew away with Shepherd Wind.

"Good-by," they said, "good-by, dear mother tree."

"Good-by," said the mother.

"I shall stay here to take care of our babies."

colder   faded   brown   fluttered
covered   scattered

*   *   *   *   *   *   *

The leaves had a fine time playing with the Wind.

But soon it grew colder. Their bright dresses became faded and brown.

They fluttered softly on the ground.

At last they fell asleep.

While they slept they covered up the seeds.

You remember that Shepherd Wind had scattered them.

The blue sky smiled down upon them.

Can you think why?

All their lives long these little leaves had
been doing good.

Even now they were helping others.

And they had had a good time too.

**Hallowe'en   November   Saints   ghosts
hinges   barrel   grinning   monster**

To-night will be Hallowe'en.

September has gone.

October is going.

November will soon be here.

Hallowe'en is the last night of October.

It is the night before All Saints' Day.

Perhaps this is why people think that ghosts
come back to earth.

Strange things certainly happen every Hallow-
e'en.

But I do not believe that they are done by
ghosts.

Would a ghost ring front door bells?

If they did, would their feet fairly rattle
down the steps?

Would ghosts take front gates from their
hinges?

Would ghosts run off with ash barrels?

Would a ghost cut the top from a pumpkin?
Would he then cut out the inside?
Would he cut out two eyes, a nose, and a mouth full of teeth?
Would he put a candle inside?
Would he put the grinning monster in a dark place?
Perhaps.
But it was a boy who did all this *last* year.

OCTOBER'S PARTY

**October   hundreds   carpet   crimson
scarlet**

October gave a party;
    The leaves by hundreds came,
From Chestnuts, Oaks, and Maples,
    From trees of every name.

The sunshine spread a carpet,
    And everything was grand;
Miss Weather led the dancing,
    Professor Wind the band.

The Chestnuts came in yellow,
  The Oaks in crimson dressed,
The lovely Misses Maple
  In scarlet looked their best.

Professor Wind played louder;
  They flew along the ground,
And then the party ended
  In hands across, all round.

— From Song Stories for Little Folks.

NOVEMBER

"November's sky is chill and drear,
November's leaf is red and sere."

— Sir Walter Scott.

THE ENGLISH SPARROW

sparrow   throat   mate   people   breakfast
dinner   supper   beak   nostrils

This is Mr. Sparrow.
Look at the black mark on his throat.
Do you see the white bar on the wings?
Mrs. Sparrow has a gray throat.
She has no white on her wing.
She is not as pretty as her mate.
But the baby Sparrows look like her.

Mr. and Mrs. Sparrow like to eat corn.

The Sparrow children eat the same thing.

Do you not think it is hard food for such little people?

Would you like to eat hard seeds for your breakfast, dinner, and supper?

But then you have not a strong beak to crush the grains.

The sparrow has two eyes, two nostrils, two ears, two arms, two legs.

Its nostrils are in its beak.

His ears are behind the eyes.

But where are his arms?

slender　　chirp　　scold

Here is Mr. Sparrow again.

Look at his feet.

Now you see why his toes are so long.

But are they not in the way when he tries to walk?

He does not walk; he hops.

Why is he called an English sparrow?

Because he was brought here from England.
We have many sparrows of our own.
They are not more beautiful, perhaps.
But some of them have very beautiful voices.
The English sparrow can chirp.
He cannot sing.
He can only scold.

———◆———

THE SPARROW AGAIN

nuisance   country   chatter   caterpillar
different   damage   prosper

The English sparrow is a nuisance in the country.

He fights with the smaller birds.

He keeps up a chatter that bothers the larger ones.

And he eats a great deal of fruit. He will seldom touch a caterpillar.

But in the city it is different.

No other birds will stay there.

So people are glad to have even the sparrow.

To be sure, he does some damage.

He sometimes eats the young tree buds.

But then, he sometimes eats a caterpillar too.

If it were not for the English sparrow, some people would never see a bird.

"So here is to his good health, and all his family's.

"May they live long, and prosper."

THE SPARROW'S NEST.

Nay, only look what I have found!
A sparrow's nest upon the ground;
A sparrow's nest, as you may see,
Blown out of yonder old elm tree.

And what a medley thing it is!
I never saw a nest like this, —
Not neatly wove with tender care,
Of silvery moss and shining hair;

But put together, odds and ends,
Picked up from enemies and friends;
See, bits of thread, and bits of rag,
Just like a little rubbish-bag!

—MARY HOWITT.

farewell   butterfly   welcomed

Fly away, butterfly,
  Fly away home ;
The summer is going,
  And autumn has come.

The asters are blooming,
  The nuts are all ripe,
Jack Frost comes to see us
  Almost every night.

So fly away, butterfly,
  Fly far away
To the land where the sunshine
  And sweet roses stay.

And when, in the spring time,
  The sunshine is here,
You must return
  And be welcomed, my dear.

— *Youth's Companion.*

WHICH WAY DOES THE WIND BLOW?

o'er valley height traverse flight
rages whither

Which way does the wind blow,
And where does he go?
He rides o'er the water
And over the snow;
O'er wood and o'er valley,
And over the height —
Where goats cannot traverse
He taketh his flight.

He rages and tosses,
And bare is the tree,
As when you look upward
You plainly can see —
But from whence he comes,
Or whither he goes,
There is no one can tell you,
There is no one who knows.

— MARY LAMB.

covered   people   Eskimos
smother   reason

There is to the north of us a land called
Greenland.

It ought to be called Whiteland or Snowland.

For most of the year it is covered with snow.

Here live the people called Eskimos.

They build houses from blocks of snow.

These are much warmer than you would
think.

Perhaps the Eskimo learned how warm they
were from the white bear.

Just before winter the white bear lies down.
She waits until the snow covers her all over..
The snow gets deeper and deeper.
But the white bear's warm body melts out a
hollow place.
Here she lives all winter long without food.
And her babies live with her.
Perhaps you think that they would smother.
No; the snow is full of air.
That is the reason that it is so white.
And then the wind blows softly through it.

**hurrying   creatures   greeted   under-
ground   buried   treasures**

How gray the trees look!
And the earth, too, is hard and bare.
There are no ants hurrying along.
No grasshoppers fly out of the grass.
We no longer hear the "croak! croak!
croak!" of the frogs.
We do not hear the "hum! hum!" of the
bees.
All through the autumn living creatures
greeted us at every step.
But now all is still.

Where have they gone?

Are they dead?

The ants have gone to their underground home.

The grasshoppers are mostly dead.

But they have left their eggs carefully buried in the ground.

The frogs have hidden themselves in the mud.

They have begun their long winter nap.

The honey bees are in their hives.

Mrs. Wasp and Mrs. Bumble Bee are hiding under logs or stones, or in cracks.

It seems as if all life was dead, it is true.

But life is only asleep.

Soon the buds and seeds and eggs and cocoons will open.

And in the spring we shall again see the treasures that these dear boxes hold.

pupa   finished   safely

Why, what is this?

Is it a bud?

Let us open it to see.

There are no little leaves inside.

But there is plenty of loose silk.

Then comes another tough wall.

 And in the inner room we find this.

What is it?

It is called a pupa, and it was once a caterpillar, just like this: —

The caterpillar made his own house.

You should have seen him at work.

Spin! Spin! Spin!

At last when it was finished he went to sleep.

What a fine house he has made.

See the shiny outside covering.

Do you think that the Rain can get in?

If he did he could not get through the next wall.

What a warm little home it is.

I think that the Pupa may safely sleep in it all winter long.

Don't you?

THE SILK WORM

silk worm   mulberry   threads   coffin

Silk worm on the mulberry tree
Spin a silken robe for me;
Draw the threads out fine
   and strong,
Longer yet — and very
   long;
Longer yet — 'twill
   not be done
Till a thousand
   more are spun.
Silk worm, turn
   this mulberry tree
Into silken threads
   for me!

Spinning ever! now 'tis done,
Silken threads enough are spun!
Spinning, they will spin no more —
All their little lives are o'er!
Pile them up — a costly heap! —
Each in his coffin gone to sleep!

Silk worm on the mulberry tree,
Thou hast spun and died for me !
— MARY HOWITT.

**hyacinth   cradle   jackets
waterproof   onion**

I am a hyacinth bulb.

The ground was my cradle.

All summer long I grew and grew and grew.

The bigger I grew the more jackets I put on.

Now I have a dozen jackets.

Outside of these I wear a waterproof coat.

See what a beautiful flower is inside me.

I am protecting it from the cold and damp of winter !

I have many cousins.

They take care of their little flowers in the same way.

The lilies are my cousins, and the tulips too.

Some people do not like my cousin the onion.

They think that her odor is too strong.

But she is very good to eat, if it were not for that.

potato   woman   cellar   pieces

I was born in the ground too.
But I am not a tulip bulb.

Oh, no! I am the old woman who lived in the shoe.

For I have so many children that I don't know what to do.

They are such strong little children.

They do not wait to be put in the ground.

They will begin to grow even in the cellar.

You can cut me into pieces.

Then each of these eyes will be a potato plant.

And what will the potato plant do all summer?

Why, make other potatoes, to be sure.

Perhaps you think that potato plants are grown for you.

Not at all.

They are grown for the little potato children.

For the potato children like to eat the potato as well as you.

THE BEAR

autumn   eating   honey   fonder   watching

I spend my winter in the ground too.

But I am not a bulb either.

Nor am I a po-tato.

I am Mr. Bear.

All autumn long, I have been eating, eating, eating.

And of what do you suppose I have eaten the most.

F

Why, of honey, to be sure.

I am fonder of honey than any little child.

And I can eat more too.

It does not make me ill to eat a very great deal of sweet.

I am always watching for bees' nests.

I am very fat now.

I do not feel like working any more.

The other day I found a beautiful den, under the rocks.

I have been lining it with moss and leaves and pine branches.

Is is very warm and comfortable inside.

I believe that I could spend a very happy winter sleeping there.

So good-by, until April!

———◆———

THE RISING MOON

**watching   surely   rising   higher
happen   dreadful**

Ah, the moon is watching me!
White and round as round can be,
Over the house and the top of the tree,

Rising slowly,
We shall see
Something happen
Very soon.
Hide me from the dreadful moon.

Slowly, surely, rising
higher;
Soon she will be as
high as the spire!
It seems as if something must happen then
To all the world and all the men!
Oh, I dare not think,
For I am not wise;
I must look away,
I must shut my eyes.

— *From Lilliput Levee.*

THE MOON

silver   middle   fairy   golden

But the moon is not always large and white
and round.

Sometimes it
looks like a tiny
silver boat.

How would
you like to sit in
the middle of it?

How would you like to sail around all night
long?

Perhaps the sky is a great blue lake.

And perhaps the stars are water lilies.

And perhaps you are a little fairy.

And perhaps
— but look, the
moon is no longer
a boat!

And where are
you?

You must have fallen down to the earth
again!

*   *   *   *   *   *   *

The round moon is called the full moon.

The little boat is called the new moon.

Then there is the half moon.

Indeed, there are two half moons.

After the new moon comes the first half moon.

And after the full moon comes the last half moon.

Even the full moon is not as bright as the sun.

We say the golden sun.

But we say the silver moon.

WHY WE HAVE THANKSGIVING

**English   Massachusetts   Pilgrims
harvest   blessings**

Many years ago a hundred English people came to settle in Massachusetts.

They were called the Pilgrims.

Perhaps you have heard of our Pilgrim Fathers?

It was December when they reached this country.

Some rough log houses were built.

But the weather was very cold.

The snow fell fast and often.

They did not have enough of the right kind of food.

So first one was taken sick and then another.

But in the spring they planted plenty of corn.

Summer brought the sunshine to ripen it.

So when autumn came they had a fine harvest.

They had given thanks every day for their blessings.

But they wanted to have a big Thanksgiving.

THE FIRST THANKSGIVING

dinner   pumpkins   turkey
deer   goodness

The Pilgrims invited the Indians to their first Thanksgiving dinner.

The mothers made pies out of the pumpkins.

They made bread and cakes from the corn.

The Pilgrim fathers went hunting and fishing.

What do you think that they found?

A GREAT WILD TURKEY!

And the Indians brought a present of five large deer.

They were dressed in their very best.

They had on plenty of paint and snakes and fox tails.

Both Pilgrims and Indians thanked God for his goodness to them.

In the evening they sang and danced.
They ran races and played games too.
They tried to see who could shoot farthest.
They must have had a good time.
For they stayed three whole days.
And this happened nearly three hundred years ago.

ANOTHER THANKSGIVING.

oysters   helped   **playthings**   **stalks**
soldier

The Pilgrims did not always have so much to eat on Thanksgiving Day.

But they always tried to be happy and thankful on that day.

One year they had nothing but some oysters and a very little corn.

They put the oysters and five grains of corn on each plate.

And they were glad that they had even this little food.

That was their least happy Thanksgiving.

So ever after they put five grains of corn at each plate every Thanksgiving.

It showed them how much more they had to be thankful for.

Some people still put the five grains at each Thanksgiving plate.

* * * * * * *

Even the little Pilgrim children were very fond of corn.

They had no toys.

They had to make their own playthings.

Out of the stalks they made guns.

The boys played soldier with the guns.

Then the little girls sometimes made dolls from the ears.

The silk made the hair.

Look at it on the next page.

And best of all, out of the cobs they made lovely corn cob houses.

Indians   tassel   princess   satin

The Indians thought that the corn plant was once a prince.

They believed that he came to earth to help them.

The tassel was the feather of his cap.

The silk was his golden hair.

The leaves made his green dress.

Corn is even beautiful enough to be a princess.

Have you seen the long slender leaves shining like satin in the sun?

Perhaps the tassel was the feather in a prince's cap.

But what is it now?

It is the flower of the corn.

The corn has two kinds of flowers.

The tassel is one kind, and makes the flower dust.

All flowers have to have this dust to make the seeds.

But where are the seeds?

Not at the top on the tassel.

No; they are on the corn cob below.

Take off the husk from the corn.

See how the silk comes from the grains.

But sometimes there is silk and no grain of corn.

Shepherd Wind did not carry the flower dust to this thread of silk.

But he does his work well on the whole.

And so most ears of corn are full of grains.

DECEMBER

" And dull December brings to earth
    That time which gave our Savior birth."

" The year is done — Let all revere
    The great good Father of the year."

— MARY HOWITT.

THE THREE LITTLE GOLDFISH

crumbs   remember   lattice   frightened

There was once a man who had three gold-fish.

Every day he threw crumbs to them

The fish would swim quickly to the top to eat the crumbs.

Then the good man would say : —

" Dear little goldfish, remember two things.

" Never swim through the lattice into the big pond.

" And never go up the bank when I am not here."

The little fish did not understand.

So the man went down and stood near the lattice.

Whenever the fish swam near the lattice, he beat the water with a stick.

This frightened the fish away.

He did the same thing when they came to the bank.

But still the fish did not understand.

* * * * * * *

" He is on top himself," said one little fish.

" He does not love us. He does not want us to have a good time," said another.

" I shall not mind him," said the first fish.

" I shall go right off to the big pond."

" I shall not mind him either," said the second.

" I am going upon the bank to enjoy the beautiful sunshine."

But the third little goldfish stayed down in the deep water.

He did not know why the man told him to do so. He only knew that the man loved him.

But what do you think happened?

When the first fish came to the big pond, a great fish ate him up.

The second little fish died on the bank.

And only the third little fish was left alive.

He lived for a long time in the clear water of the beautiful pond.

— Adapted from LA FONTAINE.

THE GOLDFISH

eyelids   breathing   gill covers

Here is the Goldfish

He has two eyes, a nose, a mouth, a pair of arms, and a pair of legs.

He has no eyelids.

But he can move his eyes.

His nose is hard to find.

Just like your nose, it is above the mouth.

But he does not use these small holes for breathing.

He breathes through his mouth and gill covers.

The water goes into his mouth and out past the gills.

But water is not air.

No; but there is air in it.

Have you never watched the water boil?

Then you have seen the air coming out of it.

G

It is easy enough to find a fish's mouth.

He opens and shuts it all day long.

It is no wonder. For he has to breathe and eat with it.

How does the fish move?

Just as our little baby creeps.

He uses both his hands and feet.

To be sure we do not call them hands and feet.

We call them fins.

They are not just like hands and feet either.

But then a fish lives in the water.

Perhaps if we had to swim all day long our hands would be like fins too.

aquarium   tadpole   mussel   covering

Are these animals fish too?

They live in the aquarium with the fish.

The first one is called a tadpole.

But then the shad is not called a fish either.

The Tadpole has two eyes, nose, mouth and tail.

And so has the fish.

But the tadpole has no arms nor legs.

But perhaps that does not matter.

Wait until spring, and then we shall see.

These other animals do not look at all like a fish.

One of them is a snail, and the other a mussel.

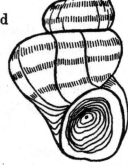

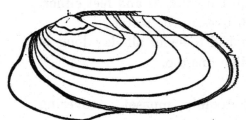

Both of them have very strange coverings.

The snail carries his house with him.

But it is very light.

His body is so soft that he needs a shell to protect him.

But how does the mussel get around with his heavy house?

He cannot move quite so quickly as the snail.

But he has a foot, and walks mostly at night.
The long marks in the sand are made by
his foot.

THE SPRUCE TREE

snowflakes   evergreens   branches   cones

See the snowflakes on the spruce tree!
Do they not look pretty on the green leaves?

By and by the wind will shake them off.

The spruce tree does not mind keeping them until then.   Her branches are tough.

The spruce tree is one of the evergreens.

They do not mind Jack Frost nor the northwest wind.

All winter long they keep their green leaves.

But these leaves are not like those of other trees.

They are long and slender.

They are called needles.

And here are the flowers of the spruce.

They are called cones.

But in each scale there are two pretty winged seeds.

And this is one reason why all birds love evergreen trees.

Do you ever go bird hunting in winter?

If you do, then watch the evergreen trees.

OTHER EVERGREENS

**balsam fir   rounder   pointed   Christmas
mistletoe**

There are many kinds of evergreens.

Here is the balsam fir!

It looks very much like
a spruce.

But its branches are flatter,
and its needles less pointed.

Both the spruce and balsam fir
are used for Christmas.

Notice whether your Christmas tree is a spruce
or a fir.

And here are some other Christmas greens : —

This is the holly.   And this is the mistletoe.

The mistletoe grows on other trees.

It keeps them green after they have lost their own green leaves.

These trees would look dead if it were not for the green mistletoe.

Perhaps this is the reason that it is used at Christmas.

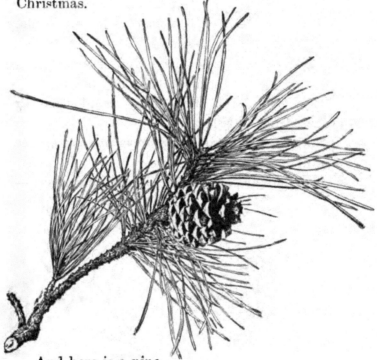

And here is a pine.

They have the longest needles of all.

THE FIR TREE

wood cutters   autumn   slender   scarcely

In the forest stood a pretty fir.

She was not alone.

Pines and other firs grew around her.

So she had plenty of friends, and sunshine, and air.

But she was not happy.

She wanted to be taller.

In the autumn each year the wood cutters came to cut a few of the largest trees.

They cut off their branches.

This made them look long and slender.

The fir tree scarcely knew them.

Then she trembled lest she should be cut down too.

But she kept asking herself : —

" Where are they going ?

" What will happen to them ? "

swallows   storks   masts

In the spring the fir tree asked the swallows and storks : —

"Did you not meet the trees that were taken from the woods?

"Do you not know where they are?"

The stork said : —

"Yes, I think so.

"As I flew back from the south, I met many new ships.

"These ships had tall masts.

"They smelt like fir.

"And I am sure those were the trees."

"Oh," said the fir, "if I were only big enough to go over the sea!"

The wind kissed the little fir tree.

The dew shed tears upon her.

But the poor little fir tree did not understand.

candles   fastened   garret

At last it was Christmas.

The wood cutters came to the woods again.

This time they cut down the younger trees.

They did not cut off the branches.

The little fir tree was carried away with the others.

And just what some sparrows had told her came true.

Bags of candy were hung on her branches.

Golden apples and nuts hung down as if they grew there.

Dolls and toys were on the tree.

A hundred candles were fastened to her branches.

" This is splendid," thought the little fir tree.

But some of the pretty things were taken from her.

They were given to the happy children.

At last the candles were put out.

The people went to bed, leaving the poor little tree all alone.

In the morning she was carried to the garret.

beginning   servant   chopped   underneath

Days and nights went by.

Nobody came to see the fir.

She was very unhappy.

But at last the tree was brought to the light again.

" Now life is beginning again," said the fir tree.

She felt the fresh air and the sunbeams.

She saw again the lovely flowers.

Two children were playing in the yard.

When one of them saw the tree, she said : —

" Oh, look at that old fir tree ! "

The tree looked at the flowers.

Then she looked at herself.

How she wished that she had stayed in the forest !

Soon a servant chopped the little tree into pieces.

They made a bright blaze underneath the tea-kettle.

And at last the tree was all burned up !

— *Adapted from* HANS ANDERSEN.

—◆—

" Over the river and through the wood
  To grandfather's house we go.
    The horse knows the way
    To carry the sleigh
  Through the white and drifted snow."

DAISIES

**evening   meadow   dreaming   picked
dropped**

At evening, when I go
  to bed,
I see the stars shine
  overhead.
They are the little
  daisies white
That dot the meadows
  of the night.

And often, while I'm dreaming so,
Across the sky the moon
  will go.
She is a lady, sweet and fair,
Who comes to gather dai-
  sies there.

For when, in the morning, I arise,
There's not a star left in the skies.
She's picked them all and dropped
  them down
Into the meadows of the town.

        — FRANK DEMPSTER SHERMAN.

THE STARS

midnight   usually   impossible   happily

Up in Greenland there is but one day and but one night in the whole year.

The short day is summer.

The long night is winter.

When it is midnight here it is usually very dark.

But in Greenland, in summer, the sun shines at midnight.

All day and all night he shines, for many weeks.

This does not seem at all strange to the little Eskimo children.

They have never known anything else.

They would think it very strange to see a moon and stars that shone only at night.

And a sun that hid itself at night, even in summer, — "Oh, that is impossible!" they would say.

We know that the silver moonlight is only sunlight, after all.

But what is true about the stars?

Can you believe some of the stars are suns?

Other stars move around them, just as our earth moves around the sun.

Suppose that you were living on one of these other earth stars.

Suppose that it was a clear, clear night.

Could you see our earth?

Perhaps, if you were not too far off.

But even then it would only be a tiny, tiny star.

Some of our largest and brightest stars are earth stars.

Perhaps people and other animals, and plants even, live happily on them.

★ ✳ **Pole Star**

Little Dipper

Great Dipper

NORTHWEST WIND

swallows   squirrel   chimney   coal bins

Winter is here at last!
The trees are bare.
Most of the birds have left us.
There are no flowers to be found.
Jack Frost has come.
And the Northwest Wind is here to stay!
He says : —
" Run away, winds of the south and west.
" Go where the swallows are, south wind.
" Follow the sunset, west wind.
" These are my months."
So he runs after his brothers over the lakes.
He rolls up the waves, and gives them white
caps to wear.
" Are you strong?" he cries to the trees.
" How thick is your wool?" he says to the
sheep.
" Have you found your winter nest?" he says
to the squirrel.
He slams the door.
He shakes the window.

He howls down the chimney: "Are your coal bins full?"

To everybody he has said:—

" Get ready, for winter is coming!

" Are you ready? for winter is here."

JACK FROST

loveliest   canvas   painted   destroys

Jack Frost likes best to work at night.

Then he paints his loveliest pictures.

His canvas is a pane of glass.

His paint is always white.

But he draws so well that the color does not matter.

Look at this picture that he painted for me last night.

This is the grass, and here are the trees.

It looks like winter.

But there are birds in the sky.
All of the people are dressed in finest lace.
Perhaps they are going to the church.
Quick!   Here is the sun.
He does not like Jack Frost.
He destroys his pictures.

TINY LITTLE SNOWFLAKES

angles	floating	whirling	dancing
kissing	loading	powdering	cunning

Tiny little snowflakes
In the air so high,
Are you little angels
Floating in the sky?

Whirling on the sidewalk,
Dancing in the street,
Kissing all the faces
Of the children sweet,

Loading all the housetops,
Powdering all the trees —
Cunning little snowflakes,
Little busy bees.

—LUCY LARCOM.

H

SNOWFLAKES

whenever   frightened   comfort   noticed

Who makes the snowflakes? Why, Jack Frost, to be sure.

He changes water to ice wherever he goes.

When he touches a raindrop it freezes into ice.

Then it falls to the earth.

We do not call it a raindrop, then.

We call it hail.

But sometimes Jack Frost gets hold of the clouds before the raindrops are born.

Then he freezes the water, too.

He makes long, thin needles.

Perhaps the little ice needles are frightened at the change.

Perhaps each tries to comfort the other.

At any rate you will always find six of them together.

All these lovely snowflakes have six parts.

But they all seem to be of the same size.

This is not the case.

In what kind of weather do we have the largest flakes?

Gather some flakes on a black cloth.

Then you will see why some flakes are larger than others.

JACK FROST AGAIN

fellow   visits   sparkling   carpet

Jack Frost is a queer little fellow.

He comes to us first in the autumn.

But he only makes short visits.

He comes, too, only in the night-time.

But even then he works hard.

What does he do?

He helps to color the leaves.

Then he helps them to fall from the trees.

If it were not for Jack Frost they would fall one by one.

Then how lonely they would be!

He helps to open the chestnut burrs.

If it were not for Jack Frost, Shepherd Wind could not sow so many seeds.

When winter comes Jack Frost makes longer visits.

In many places he stays all winter long.

Then, of course, he does more work. ·

He covers the fields with a sparkling carpet.

He puts a glass roof over the brooks.

He makes slides for the children.

But best of all he makes the snowflakes.

Why do we say best of all?

Perhaps, because from snow you can make fine snowballs and snow men.

That is great fun, but that is not all.

The snow is a warm, warm blanket.

It covers the green grass and tender plants.

Without the snow we could not have spring.

CLOTHES

winter   feathers   scales   swimming

Who likes cold weather?

Suppose that you had to wear your summer clothes in winter.

Then it would not be so fine.

Other animals have summer clothes.

The trees have more clothes in summer than in winter.

That would not suit us.

But then we are not trees.

*   *   *   *   *   *   *

Look at the bird on the other page.

See what a fine dress she has.

How soft and light it is!

It will not be too heavy to carry as she flies.

It will help her to fly.

*   *   *   *   *   *   *

Now look at the fish.

His dress is not of feathers.

They would get wet and heavy in the water.

Dress a fish in feathers.

What would become of him?

A fish's dress is made of hard, shiny scales.

They lap over.

The water cannot get in.

They are oiled.

No wonder the fish can slip easily through the water.

His body can bend easily in swimming.

How could he have a better dress?

And yet what could a bird do with a fish's dress?

JANUARY

"Snowballs showering,
  Snow men towering,
Fingers tingling,
  Sleigh-bells jingling,
Horns a-tooting,
That's our merry
January."

— *From Youth's Companion.*

THE LITTLE NEW YEAR

**tripping   shaking   din   blessings
treasure**

Oh, I am the little New Year, oh, ho!
Here I come tripping it over the snow,
Shaking my bells with a merry din,
So open your doors and let me in!

Blessings I bring for each and all,
Big folks and little folks, short and tall;
Each from me a treasure may win,
So open your doors and let me in.

For I am the little New Year, oh, ho!
Here I come tripping it over the snow,
Shaking my bells with a merry din,
So open your doors and let me in.

—From Youth's Companion.

LINDU, THE KEEPER OF THE BIRDS

**finished   hunters   Northern Light
jewels**

The world was finished.
God made beautiful Lindu.
He gave her charge of all the birds.
Sometimes the hunters tried to shoot these
birds.
Then Lindu sent a stormy wind.
This blew dust in their eyes.
The North Star wished to marry her.
But Lindu would not let him.
" You always stay in one place," she said.
" I do not love you."
Then the moon asked her to marry him.
To him she said : —
" You change your face too often.
" Besides, you always travel the same road."
She said the same thing to the sun.
Then the Northern Light came to her.
A thousand white horses drew his diamond
coach.
His servants carried a cloak full of jewels.
Lindu loved this bright and changeful one.

She promised to marry
him when the swallows
flew south.

A mountain stream
sent her a bridal veil.

The Frost King
sent her laces.

They were very
beautiful and fine.

A breath of sum-
mer air would de-
stroy them.

The birds — her own
dear birds — brought
her velvet dresses of butterflies' wings.

Her sandals were from bees' wings.

Spring passed away.

Summer came and went.

The swallows flew south.

But the Northern Light did not come to
Lindu.

But still she loved him, — not the north star,
nor the sun, nor the moon.

THE MILKY WAY

**strange   stolen   beloved   unkindness
changeful**

Poor Lindu wept.
From her tears sprang the little brooks.
The birds tried to comfort her.
Then they flew away.
They built their nests in all kinds of strange places.
Many an egg was lost.
Many a baby bird was stolen.
And all because Lindu did not help the birds.
Then the winds took pity on Lindu.
They lifted her gently from the ground.
They carried her to the sky.
And there she still lives.
Her bridal veil spreads from one end of the sky to the other.
Lift your eyes to the Milky Way.
It is Lindu in her bridal dress.
From there she directs her beloved birds.
From there she waves her white hand to the Northern Light.
She has forgotten his unkindness.

She is always beautiful and always young.
And she smiles gently at the changeful Northern Light.

— From the Russian.

WHITE LAMBKINS

Who has the whitest lambkins?
　Look up into the sky.
It is the moon, the pretty moon,
　Whose home is up on high.

She rises in the evening,
　When little children sleep;
Comes from her little cottage
　And calls her little sheep.

She calls them out to pasture
　Upon her meadows gay;
The stars are her white lambkins,
　They're never seen by day.[1]

— From the German.

[1] From *Kindergarten Chimes*. By permission of Messrs. The
Oliver Ditson Company.

THE WOODPECKER

tool · chisel   hammer   woodpecker
grub   tongue

Some birds are carpenters.

They make the strongest homes of all the birds.

But instead of building it, they bore it out.

They have only one tool.

This is both a chisel and a hammer.

They carry it always with them.

Look at this carpenter.

His name is Mr. Woodpecker.

But where is his chisel?
Yes, it is his beak.
They find a soft place
in a tree trunk.

And with their chisel beak, they chip away the soft wood.

But where is the hammer, you say.

The hammer is the bird's head.

With this he drives the chisel.

His beak helps him to get his dinner, too.

He hammers and pecks at the bark.

At last he finds a grub.

Poor little grub!

He thought that he had found a safe winter home.

Mr. Woodpecker darts out his tongue.

And that is the end of the grub.

———◆———

THE CROW'S CHILDREN

**carrying   answered   worry   astonished
parent**

A farmer was going about the field carrying a gun.

On a tree near by sat a black, black crow.

" Caw! caw! caw!" said the crow.

"What do you want?" answered the farmer.

"You must not kill my children," said the crow.

The farmer answered : —

"I shall only kill the birds that eat my crops.

"If your children have done so, I shall certainly kill them."

"Oh, my children are the best in the world.

"Not one of them would steal corn."

"But how shall I know which they are?" asked the farmer.

"Do they look like you?"

"Oh, no, they are pretty, and very white," answered the crow.

The farmer went off.

All day long his gun was heard in the field.

But the old crow did not worry.

At night the farmer came back.

A string of crows hung down his back.

"Alas," said the crow, "what have you done?

"You promised to spare my pretty birds.

"But you have killed every one of them."

The farmer was astonished.

"Why, I found them in the corn," he said.

"Besides they are black and ugly.

"How can they be your children?"

The crow was very angry.

"Get away," she said.

"No one but a parent knows how good and beautiful are her children."

"I see," said the farmer.

THE CROW

scarecrow   speckled

Look at this Crow.

He is with us summer and winter.

I wonder what he finds to eat.

Let us look at his beak.

Perhaps that will tell us.

It is strong enough to eat corn.

Besides, farmers put scarecrows in their corn-fields.

I

The English sparrow eats corn, too.

Look at his beak.

The crow eats something besides corn.

His beak is so long.

And do you see the little hook at the end ?

The farmers tell us that he eats young birds.

He sometimes eats insects and field-mice.

At any rate, he finds plenty to eat summer and winter.

But it is only in the spring that he builds a nest.

It is very large.

It is built on sticks of red cedar-bark.

And in it Mrs. Crow lays her strong speckled green eggs.

Caw ! Caw ! Caw !
Over in the meadow,
In a nest built of sticks
Lived a black mother-crow
And her little crows six.
" Caw," said the mother,
" We caw," said the six ;
So they cawed and they called
In their nests built of sticks.

— OLIVE A. WADSWORTH.

THE CAT

thicker   whiskers   windows   stretch

Many other animals stay with us all the year.
First there is the cat.
Who ever heard of a cat hiding in the ground just because it was cold?
Who ever heard of a cat going south?
But it does get a little thicker fur.
Rub the cat's back.
Do you feel something hard?
That is the cat's backbone.
She has two eyes, a nose, two ears, and a mouth.
Then there are the whiskers.
You have not got whiskers yet!
What fine eyes she has!
She can see with them at night even.
The black windows in her eyes can stretch.
So her eyes get a great deal of light.

They get enough to see even in the dark.

And then her tongue!

It is a tongue, a spoon, and a comb, — all in one.

She uses her paws for combs sometimes.

If she sees a mouse, in a moment her paw is like this.

When she wants to walk softly, her paws are like this.

As a little girl said once : —

" Oh, pussy has pins on her feet!"

A KITTEN RHYME

See my kitty,
Little Dot.
Very pretty,
Is she not?

Soft and silky
  Is her fur.
If you stroke it
  She will purr.

Often when my
  Grandma knits,
Close beside her
  Kitty sits.

Watching, watching
  Grandma's ball,
Wishing she would
  Let it fall.

When it does drop
  Oh! the fun!
You should see
  How Dot can run!

Dot has never
  Caught a rat.
She's too little
  Yet for that.

She is only
  Good at play,
But she'll catch
  The rats some day.

— EMILIE POULSSON.

THE HORSE

forehead   direction   blinders   reader

A fish, a bird, a cat, and a boy all look something alike.

They all have two eyes and two ears.

Each has a nose, a mouth, a backbone, two arms, and two legs.

But the boy's forehead and chin stand out more.

In other animals the mouth stands out more.

Here is an animal with more mouth than forehead.

We all know him and love him, too.

Look at his head.

He uses his lips for feelers.

You remember the cat has whiskers for this.

With his eyes he can see in any direction.

That is why we put blinders on him.

Did you ever see such big finger nails?

Have you ever seen any wild horses?
They are very wise, too.
They live in herds together.
The biggest and strongest of them is the
leader.
They do exactly what he tells them.
They travel with the colt and weak horses
in the middle.
Outside of these are the big strong horses.

THE COW

**vegetables   bran mash   pasture   camels
reindeer   peculiar**

All winter the cow has been eating hay.
The farmer has given her some salt, too.
Often she has eaten vegetables and bran mash
And this food has made the milk.
Think what nice milk it will be in the spring.
Then the cow goes to pasture.
Quickly she bites off the grass and clover.
She eats it too fast to chew it.
So she packs it away in a big bag.
This she keeps inside of her large body.

Later in the day she sits down to rest.

Then what she has eaten comes up in her mouth.

Only a little ball comes up at a time.

This she chews, and chews, and chews.

This is what is called "chewing the cud."

Sheep and reindeer and camels all do the same thing.

These all have peculiar feet.

Look at the cow's hoofs.

See if you can tell me something about them.

Does a horse chew his cud?

Why do you think so?

THE COW AGAIN

Perhaps the nicest thing that the cow gives us is milk.

But it is not the only thing.

Think of all that is made from milk.

I do not mean junkets and other nice desserts.

I mean butter and cheese.

It would be hard to find a part of the cow that is not useful.

From her horns are made buttons and combs.

Her hair is mixed with mortar for plaster.

Her skin gives us shoes.

Glue is made from her hoofs.

Tallow candles and beef come from her fat and flesh.

And the farmer even uses her bones.

He burns them.

Then he spreads them over the ground.

They make the soil much richer.

Do you wonder that the farmer takes such good care of his cows?

THE JANUARY THAW

crystal   trickle   vain   admired   angry

One year the winter was very, very cold.

The Ice on the pond grew thick and strong.

He was beautiful and smooth..

He thought himself a crystal floor.

And so he looked down upon the water below.

One day he said : —

"I wish that you would go some other way.

"I do not like to hear your trickle, trickle."

"But I wish," said the water, "that you would give me more room. I — I —"

His voice got thinner and thinner.

Jack Frost was making the Ice thicker and thicker all the time.

One day the skaters came.

They all said: —

"What lovely Ice!"

And the Ice grew more vain.

In the evening the snowflakes came.

They said to themselves: —

"How we shall be admired in the morning!"

In the morning the Ice was very angry.

For the snowflakes covered him up.

quarrel   angrily   poured

"Who sent you?" the Ice asked the snowflakes.

"Nobody," answered they.

"The clouds were too heavy to carry us.

"So some of us came down.

"You should be glad to see us.

"The wind and the skies all love us."

"If they love you let them take you away," said the Ice, angrily.

Then the water began to quarrel with them both.

Were there ever three such silly people as Ice, Water, and Snow.

I wish that I could say no!

At last the wind changed to the south.

And the thaw came.

The Ice grew thinner and thinner.

Then the water poured over it.

The snow heaps fell in.

They all rolled about together.

They cried: —

"What have we been doing?

"Friends, dear friends, we are all of us brothers together."

And they hugged each other closely.

No one could say: —

"This was Ice.

"Or this was Snow.

"Or this was never anything but Water."

And so it is to this day.

—Adapted from Mrs. Gatty.

FIVE PEAS IN A POD

watered   forever   earthquake

Once there were five peas growing in a pod.
The peas were green.
The vine was green.
The leaves were green.
So the five peas thought that all the world
was green.
The warm sun shone on the vine.
The summer rain watered it.
Both the pod and the peas grew bigger and
bigger.
" Are we to lie here forever ? " said one.
" I am tired of it," said another.
" I am afraid that we shall become hard," said
the third.
" I want to see what there is outside," said a
fourth.
The fifth cried because he could not get
out.
At last the vine turned yellow.
The pod turned yellow.
The peas turned yellow.

"All the world is turning yellow," said the peas with one voice.

Then there came an earthquake.

The pod burst open with a crack.

All five peas rolled into the yellow sunshine.

**caught   pea-shooter   sprouted
famously**

A boy caught all the five peas.

He put the biggest one in his pea-shooter.

Then he shot it out.

"Catch me if you can," said the big pea.

"I shall fly straight into the sun," said the next one.

"I shall travel farthest," said the third pea.

"Let me alone," said the fourth.

"What is to be, will be," said the fifth pea.

He landed in an empty flower-pot.

This flower-pot was in the window of a sick girl's room.

The pea sprouted.

It grew into a beautiful vine.

"Dear mother, I think that I shall get well," said the little girl one day.

"For my pea is growing famously."

"I hope so," said the mother.

She put a stick into the pot.

This was so that the vine might cling to it.

After many days there was a beautiful pea blossom.

It smiled in the sunshine.

The little girl kissed it softly, and said : —

"Now I am sure that I am going to get well."

—Adapted from HANS CHRISTIAN ANDERSEN.

FEBRUARY

And this is February!
He is the last and shortest of winter children.
He is the baby of the year.
I think his mother must like him.
For every four years she gives him an extra day
No other months have extra days.
But then in no other month was born

GEORGE WASHINGTON,

ABRAHAM LINCOLN,

and

ST. VALENTINE.

THE NORTH WIND

The North Wind doth blow,
And we shall have snow,
And what will the robin do then, poor thing?
He'll sit in a barn,
And keep himself warm,
And hide his head under his wing, poor thing.

The North Wind doth blow,
And we shall have snow,
And what will the swallow do then, poor thing?
Oh do you not know,
He has gone long ago,
To a country much warmer than ours, poor
    thing?

The North Wind doth blow,
And we shall have snow,
And what will the dormouse do then, poor thing?
Rolled up like a ball,
In his nest snug and small,
He'll sleep till warm weather comes back, poor
    thing.   — *Old Song.*

ABRAHAM LINCOLN

BORN FEBRUARY 12, 1809

**birthday   birthplace   plough   threshed
President   thoroughly   respect**

To-day was Abraham Lincoln's birthday.
Here is a picture of his birthplace.

It was a poor cabin, with only one room.
There were no windows.
And there was only one door.
His bed was a pile of dry leaves.
His trousers were of deer skin.
His hat was a coon skin.
But he could do a great deal of work.
He could drive a team of horses.
He could handle a plough.

He threshed wheat and chopped wood.

He carried water, made the fire, and tended the baby.

When he grew up he split rails for fences.

He earned his living in many other ways too.

At last he became President of the United States.

He did this work just as thoroughly as he had done everything else.

This is why we all love and respect him.

GEORGE WASHINGTON

BORN FEBRUARY 22, 1732

plantation   **Virginia**   **wrestler**   **gourds**
obedient   **boisterous**

To-morrow will be Washington's birthday.
He was the first President of the United
States.

Would you like to hear what he was like as a little boy?

He was not poor like Lincoln.

He lived on a large plantation in Virginia.

He could ride a horse when he was nine years old.

He could swim and row.

He was the fastest runner of all the boys.

He was also the best wrestler.

At school they used to play soldier.

They had cornstalks for swords.

Their drums were gourds.

Washington's side always won.

He never did an underhand thing.

He hated a lie.

He kept his promises.

He was obedient.

But he was fond of fun.

He was as boisterous and boyish as you.

OUR WINTER VISITORS

visitors   chickadee   tinkling   carpenter saucy

Here is a bird that comes to us from the north.

He stays with us all winter.

He looks like the sparrow.

But the two long outside tail feathers are white.

He is very fond of dog kennels.

Like the sparrow, he is not afraid of us.

Even on the coldest day of winter you may hear his silver tinkling: —

Chick-a-dee-dee,
Chickadee-dee.

He is a little fellow to be a carpenter.

But his little beak is very strong.

He sometimes cuts his nest out of hard wood.

This is Jenny Wren.

It is her cousin, the Win-ter Wren, whom you saw in the snow yesterday.

They look very much alike, with their saucy tails.

Jenny goes south for the winter.

But Winter Wren comes to us from the north.

Look at his beak.

Do you think that he could break corn with it?

No; and he will not touch a crumb.

But flies and worms — these he loves.

**roast   kitchen   melting   boilers   machin-
ery   locomotives**

> "Simple Simon made a snowball
>   And brought it in to roast.
> He put it on the kitchen fire
>   And soon the ball was lost."

Have you ever seen the snow melting away out of doors?

What made it melt?

The Fairy Heat.

She has many homes.

The sun is one of them.

The stove is another.

See what Fairy Heat is doing to this water!

She is making the clouds.

These clouds are made of tiny, tiny water drops.

We might call them water dust.

How light they are!

But steam is really very strong.

He is a giant.

Men shut him up in boilers.

They give him only a little hole. Through this he escapes.

He pushes against machinery in escaping.

In this way Giant Steam runs steamboats and locomotives.

He runs mills, too.

He does many other kinds of work.

THE STORY OF A GRAIN OF WHEAT

CHAPTER I

nothing   questions   playing

A little grain of wheat lived with many other grains in a sack.

It was very dark.

No one could move about in the sack.

So there was nothing to do but to sit still and talk.

This little grain talked a great deal.

But she did not think very much.

But the grain next to it thought a great deal.

He only spoke when he was asked questions.

So we will call him the wise little grain of wheat.

One day two boys were playing near the sack.

A lady brought them something on a plate.

"It's cake! It's cake! Nice mamma for bringing us cake," they said.

Then they began to eat it and ask questions: —

"Who made the cake?"

"The cook."

"Who made the cook?"

"God."

"What did He make her for?"

"Why didn't He make her white?"

"Why didn't He make you black?"

"What is the cake made of?"

"Flour, sugar, eggs, and butter."

"What is flour made of?"

"Of wheat."

The wise little grain of wheat was frightened.

But our little grain wanted to get out of the sack.

She did not care what happened.

CHAPTER II

something common minded

After this something happened.

A man and boy moved the sack from its place.

All the little grains woke from their long nap.

" What is the matter? " said our little grain.

" Hush! " said the wise little grain.

" I think that we are going to be sown."

" What is sown? "

" It is being thrown into the earth."

" Into the earth? " cried our little grain.

" Into the common earth? "

" The earth is nothing but dirt! "

" I won't be sown!

" I would rather stay in the sack."

But just then she was carried off by the farmer.

The farmer could not hear her voice at all.

He would not have minded if he had.

He knew that she was only a grain of wheat.

He knew that she ought to be sown.

CHAPTER III

ploughed   farmer   thought

The wheat was carried into a large field.
It had just been ploughed.

So the air was full of the smell of fresh earth.

The sky was a deep, deep blue.

But the air was cool.

There were no leaves on the trees.

The farmer put his great brown hand into the bag.

He threw the little grain of wheat far from him.

Our little grain found herself in the shadow of a large warm clod of earth.

At first she thought that she was all alone.

Then she heard a voice from the other side of the clod.

It was the wise little grain of wheat.

He said : —

" We are all right so far.

" Perhaps when they cover us with earth we shall still be near."

" Do you mean to say that they will cover us with earth?"

" Yes," said the wise little grain.

" And there we shall lie in the dark.

" Then the rain will moisten us.

" And the sun will warm us.

" We shall grow larger and larger.

" And at last we shall burst open.

" Speak for yourself," said our little grain.

" I shall do nothing of the kind."

CHAPTER IV

·covered   awoke   million   together

Soon they were both covered with earth.

One morning our little grain awoke.

He found himself wet through with rain.

The next day the sun shone.

The little grain began to feel that it would have to grow larger.

For his skin was already very tight.

"Crack! Pouf! I have split all up my right side," said our little grain several days later.

"Crack! Pouf! and so have I," said the wise little grain.

"Now we must push through the earth."

"Well, I shall be glad to get into the air," said our little grain.

So each of them began to push through the earth.

The great field was brown no longer.

It was covered with a million little fresh green blades.

They grew taller and taller every day.

Our little blade grew faster than any of the others.

At last it grew into a stalk with ever so many little grains.

They fitted closely together.

They wore tight little green covers.

"Look at me," the stalk said.

"I am the queen of the wheat.

"I have a crown."

"No," said the wise little grain. "You are now an ear of wheat."

Soon all the other stalks wore a crown.

As usual the wise grain had told the truth.

CHAPTER V

color   means   happen   strange

By and bye the ears began to turn yellow.

" Yellow is the color of gold," said the little grain.

" Yes," answered the wise grain.

" But that only means that you will soon be ripe.

" You will soon be cut down.

"And then other strange things will happen."

It was just as the wise ear said that it would be.

The reaping machine came to the field.

It cut down all the ears.

These were then tied together.

They were carried in a great wagon to the barn.

Then the farmer's wife and daughters began to work very hard.

"The threshers are coming," they said, "and we must have plenty for them to eat."

The threshers came with threshing machines.

These went Puff !   Puff !   Puff !   Rattle ! Rattle ! all the time.

L

Our ear of wheat found itself grains of wheat again.

Only instead of one grain it was now many grains.

CHAPTER VI

grains   morning   foaming

All the grains of wheat were put into sacks. One morning some of our little grains heard the farmer's wife say : —

"Take this sack to the mill, Jerry.

"I want to try it for cake.

"Those city boys are very fond of cake."

So Jerry carried the sack to the wagon.

"Now we are going to travel," said our wheat.

Just then it heard two boys calling : —

"Jerry, Jerry, take us with you. We want to go to the mill."

They were the very two boys who had eaten the cake.

At last Jerry, our wheat, and the boys saw
the mill.

A big wheel was turning slowly around.

The water was dashing and foaming over it.

"What turns the wheel?" asked one of the
boys.

"The water," said Jerry.

"What turns the water."

"I don't know," said Jerry.

"What a boy you are for asking questions!"

Then he carried the wheat to the miller.

The miller put it into a hopper.

It was then crushed between two stones.

"Makes nice flour," said the miller, rubbing it
between his fingers.

CHAPTER VII

company   daughters   pea-pod

The sack of flour was carried home.

The farmer's wife opened it and said : —

"I am going to make this into cake."

Even in his wheat days the flour had never
been so proud.

"Now," it said, "I shall be rich."

The farmer's wife beat eggs and sugar and butter together in a large bowl.

Then she beat in some flour, too.

" Now, I am in grand company," said the flour.

" The eggs are the color of gold.

" The sugar is like diamonds.

" This is the company for me."

" The cake looks rich," said one of the daughters.

" I am rich, and I am a cake!" said the happy flour.

Just then a pair of brown eyes peeped into the room.

" What is that?" asked one of the boys.

" Cake."

" Who made it?"

" I did."

" I like you. You are such a nice woman. Who is going to eat any of it?"

" I am afraid it is too rich for boys."

" No," said the boy, " I am afraid it isn't."

CHAPTER VIII

oven   burned   nervous   trimmed

It was now put into a pan.

Then it went into the oven.

It was so hot in there that it nearly burned.

But it was happy again when it came out.

For every one who saw it said : —

" Oh, what a nice cake ! "

The two boys came.

They looked at it with open mouths.

This made the cake feel very nervous.

A chill ran over it.

It became quite cool.

At last the farmer's wife put it away.

She trimmed it with leaves and put it on the supper table.

It felt very happy.

But when the boys came it felt nervous again.

It almost fainted when one of them said : —

" There's the cake ! "

Then some one cut a slice.

" Go away," said the cake. " I am cake. I am rich.   I am not for boys."

But no one heard it.

Then the cake saw a red mouth open.

It opened wide enough to show two dreadful rows of little sharp, white things.

" Good gra — " began the cake.

But it never said " cious " at all.

For in a minute it was eaten.

And this is the end of the story.

———◆———

STORY OF SOME WATER DROPS

flirted　　foggy　　visit　　disappeared

Did you see the drops of water on the glass of the aquarium ?

The gold fish flirted them out with her tail.

Already they have started on their travels.

The warm air has carried them away.

By and by she will take them out of the window.

Then the sun will carry them up into the sky.

You cannot see this, of course.

For water drops are too heavy.

Even the sunbeams cannot carry them.

So first they were changed into water dust.

Do you know what water dust is ?

Now breathe into the cold air.
You can see the water dust.
Sometimes we call it steam.
When there is a great deal of water dust
around us, we say : —
"It is foggy this morning."
Our little water drops felt very happy.

They liked to travel on sunbeams.
They wanted to go to the blue sky.
After a while it was time for the sun to visit
the rest of the world.
He got red in the face over it.
But still he had to go.
So he sank lower and lower.
At last, suddenly, he disappeared.

slipped   pebbles   fanned   huddle

It grew colder and colder.
The grains of water dust were frightened.
Some of them were still near the earth.
The pebbles said : —
"Keep away from us."
But the blades of grass begged them to come
back.

So the water dust slipped down to them.

But in the morning the sun came again.

And the dew was glad to become water dust again.

It was glad to travel once more on the sunbeams.

But at noon it was very tired.

It had gone too far even to see the dear green grass.

But just then the wind took pity on it.

He fanned it with a breath into a gray cloud.

After this he blew cold again.

The little grains of water dust huddled together.

They grew larger and larger.

Patter! Clatter! Spatter! they said.

At last they came to the ground again.

And all the people said : —

"See how it rains!"

**mountain   flowed   splashed   blades
heaven**

Some of the drops fell into a mountain stream.

They clattered over the stones.

At last they reached the flour mill.

It was Jerry's mill.

And it was our little grains of wheat that they helped to grind into flour!

They had turned the wheel.

Then they flowed into a pond.

It was a beautiful pond.

On top were water lilies.

These looked like great white stars.

Below were minnows, and other pretty fish.

Every, once in a while a great green frog splashed into the water.

It was very lovely there.

So the water drops did not hurry away.

But at last they had to leave the quiet pond.

Many other brooks were tumbling down hills.

One of them was making Lindu's veil.

A beautiful broad river held out her hand to them all.

They ran to her.

And here they saw many strange sights.

They carried boats and steamers.

Over their heads were handsome bridges.

Some of the water stopped at the towns and cities, but most of it went on and on.

At last it reached the ocean.

This was the end of its earth travels.

But it went to heaven many times again.

MARCH

March is merry,
March is mad,
March is gay,
And March is sad.

—Frank Dempster Sherman

THE CROW BLACKBIRD

**colors opal rudder beechnuts
crayfish**

The blackbird is much smaller than a crow.
He is black, to be sure.
But it is a black full of colors.
He looks like a huge black opal in the sun.
There is one thing about him which is really
like the crow.
He does not hop.
He walks.

When he flies he uses his tail as a rudder.

He can pick beechnuts.

He can catch crayfish without being bitten.

Flocks of blackbirds come from the south together.

They make a great deal of noise in the early spring.

They may be seen and heard in the tops of tall trees.

Some one says : —

"Their song is like pepper and salt to the ear."

It is not a beautiful sound.

But when we hear it, we know that spring has really come.

BLUEBIRDS AND ROBINS

breast   sign   rusty   wigwam

Once upon a time there was a beautiful Indian girl.

Her name was Wenonah.

All the animals loved her.

The wild cat carried his children to her.

The deer knelt at her feet.

They wanted her to rub their heads.

The spiders spun lace for her.

But she loved the birds most of all.

The robins came first and then the bluebirds.

One night she called to them : —

"Brothers! Brothers! the time has come. I need you."

Her face shone like a star.

" I am going home," she said.

" Come with me part of the way."

She rubbed earth on the breast of each.

This was a sign that they should return to the earth.

The South Wind carried her on high.

The sun shone on the breasts of the birds.

The moist earth thus became brick red.

" Now you must return," said Wenonah.

" Wear forever the red earth color, O Robin ! "

Then she rubbed the rusty feathers on the bluebird's back.

They became blue as the sky.

" Dear, dear bluebird," she said.

" Carry on your shoulders the blue color of my new home.

" You shall be the spring sign of your Earth Mother.

"Return, my brothers," she said again.
All were weeping in the wigwam.
They said, " Wenonah is dead."
But the birds knew better.

LITTLE BIRD BLUE

Little Bird Blue, come sing us your song;
The cold winter weather has lasted so long,
We're tired of skates, and we're tired of sleds,
We're tired of snowbanks as high as our heads;
    Now we're watching for you,
    Little Bird Blue.

Soon as you sing, then the springtime will come,
The robins will call and the honey-bees hum,
And the dear little pussies, so cunning and gray,
Will sit in the willow trees over the way;
    So hurry, please do,
    Little Bird Blue !

We're longing to hunt in the woods, for we know
Just where the spring beauties and liverwort
    grow;

We're sure they will peep when they hear your
    first song,
But, why are you keeping us waiting so long,
    All waiting for you,
    Little Bird Blue?

          — *From Youth's Companion.*

M

ANOTHER STORY ABOUT ROBIN REDBREAST

Long ago in the North there was only one fire
An old man and his little son took care of it.
One day the old man became very ill.

And now the white bear watched the little
boy and the fire, too.

He wanted all the North to himself.

He saw how tired and sleepy the little boy
was becoming.

He laughed to himself.

One day the little boy fell asleep.

Then the white bear jumped on the fire with his wet feet.

He thought that he had put it out.

But a gray robin flying near knew better.

She flew down and searched until she found a tiny spark.

She fanned it with her wings.

Her little breast was burned.

But she did not give up.

At last there was a fine blaze.

Then she carried the fire to every one in the North.

The white bear went to his cave.

He growled and growled.

For now he knew that the North was not for him alone.

And this is the reason that all northern people love the robin.

------◆------

BIRD TRAVELLERS

travellers   hurry   remembers

What birds have we seen every month this year?

The sparrows and the crows, to be sure.

There are other birds, too, which stay with us all winter.

But the blackbirds left us last autumn.

They are beginning to come back again now.

While they were away we had other bird visitors.

Many of you saw the snowbirds.

Some of you heard the chick-a-dee-dee, chick-a-dee-dee.

Why do birds travel so much more than people?

Perhaps you think that they do not like the cold.

It is partly true.

But this is the real reason for the change.

When cold weather comes they cannot find enough food.

The babies are the ones that need the most food.

So it is often they who lead the others south.

How do they know how to go ?

They have never travelled before.

But in the spring it is the father who leads the way.

He is in a hurry to build his nest.

Many times he has travelled over the road.

He knows it very well, indeed.

He even remembers the tree in which he built his nest.

And he often returns to it.

———————

THE EARTHWORM

**signs   earthworm   castings   swallow
gardener**

What were the signs of spring that we found yesterday ?

They were little curly lumps of earth.

And why were some of them so wet ?

I think that it must be because they were fresh.

The curly lumps of earth are called earthworm castings.

The earthworm makes them.

Did you ever see the earthworms at work?

Sprinkle your back yard with water.

Then go out after dark.

The earthworms will be there.

They will keep their tails in their holes.

But they will be moving around and working hard.

They swallow a great deal of earth.

This is a good thing for the plants.

It makes the soil very fine.

It mixes it as a gardener would do.

Then they cover up the seeds with the castings.

The earthworm is a friend to the plants.

THE EARTHWORM AGAIN

chance   cabbage

I once heard a boy say this : —

"If you cut an earthworm in two you will have two earthworms."

Now this is not quite true.

The two parts do not die at once.

But it is only the head part that has much chance to live.

This head is not much like yours.

It has no eyes, no nose, no ears.

But it has a mouth.

The Earthworm cannot hear.

But he can feel and smell.

He even feels the light sometimes.

The Earthworm eats anything.

But he likes onions and cabbages best of all.

They must have water.

So we find them in damp places.

When it rains, they hurry from their holes.

They do not wait for the rain to come to them.

Sometimes it is very dry.

Then they go deeper and deeper in the ground.

They do this when it is cold, too.

You cannot find them then, even when you dig for them.

THE PEBBLE

knife   frightened   scratch   quartz
edges   million

I am one of the aquarium pebbles.

My home used to be in a beautiful brook.

But I like it almost as well in the aquarium.

For there are plants and animals here, too.

But one day last week something happened that I did not like.

I was put on a desk.

Behind me was a boy with a knife in his hand.

I was frightened at first.

But I need not have been.

For, try as he would, the boy could not even scratch me.

And I could scratch his knife!

The boy said that my name must be Quartz.

On the teacher's desk there was a very large piece of quartz.

It was not round and smooth.

After a while the teacher told this story about me : —

"Once upon a time this pebble was like the rock on my desk.

"But finally pieces began to break off it.

"Jack Frost did the most of this.

"But the sun and the wind and the rain all helped.

"These smaller pieces fell into a brook.

"The brook shook them all up.

"At last the edges began to wear off.

"And after many million years the rough rock became a round pebble."

A SEASHORE STORY

seashore   beach   sailor   prop   kettle

Along the seashore live many of the Quartz family.

All day long the waves roll up on the shore.

They throw the pebbles up and down.

They toss them back and forth.

They knock them against each other.

This has been going on for millions of years.

No wonder that the pebbles have grown smaller and smaller.

No wonder that near the water they are smaller still.

People call them grains of sand.

To just such a beach of sand came a strange ship one day.

This ship carried a large load of soda.

It had been on the ocean a long time.

So the sailors were glad to see the sandy beach.

They landed.

They built a fire from sticks.

But there were no stones to prop up the kettle.

The waves had worn them into sand.

So they brought soda from the ship.

At first the fire burned well.

Then suddenly something happened.

The fire melted the soda and sand together.

And for the first time glass was made.

THE WIND AND THE SUN

The North Wind and the Sun once had a dispute.

" I am stronger than you," said the North Wind.

"No, indeed," said the Sun.

"I am stronger than you, for I can do more."

Just then a man came in sight.

He was dressed in a heavy cloak.

"Let us see which of us can first take off his cloak," they said together.

The North Wind was the first to try.

He blew and blew and blew.

But the man only held the cloak more closely about him.

Then the kindly Sun first sent away the clouds that had gathered.

He sent his warmest ray straight on the man's head.

"It is very warm," said the man.

"I must take off my cloak."

This decided the question.

The Sun was right.

He could do much more than the Wind.

The Wind and the Sun had another dispute this spring.

The buds, you know, had warm, thick coats.

These were given them last autumn by the mother tree.

All winter long the wind blew and blew upon them.

But they were like the man.

They would not take off their cloaks.

No, not even when the Wind called on the snow and frost to help.

But now the warm Sun is shining on them.

And the rain is helping, too.

They are very glad to take off their warm cloaks.

———◆———

SPRING BUDS

Jack Frost and Northwest Wind will soon leave us.

Then Winter will go, too.

We shall be glad to see him go.

For we love Spring.

But we shall be glad to have winter again, too.

All winter the ground has been brown and hard.

Sometimes it has been covered with snow.

Only the evergreens have been green with leaves.

There have been no flowers and only a few birds.

Plants and animals both have been resting.

But now Spring is coming.

She will bring with her many beautiful things again.

The birds and flowers will come again.

The green grass will begin to grow.

The buds will open.

Already they are beginning to swell.

Perhaps we can fool them a little.

We will bring them indoors.

We will give them plenty of water to drink.

THE HORSE–CHESTNUT BRANCH

unfold   scales   leaflet

Look at the horse-chestnut branch.

"Then gray horse-chestnuts little
    hands unfold,
Softer than a baby's be at three
    days old."

Now you can see what was inside the tough brown scales.

Are you not glad that they were thick?

For they have kept the cold from the baby's hands.

The rain could not get in either.

No wonder that the baby's hands are soft and glossy!

Do you see the horseshoes on the branch?

How many nails do you count?

Last year the leaves were here.

Each little leaflet left a nail mark.

Do you see the rings below?

Here the scales of last year's buds fell off.

It is easy to tell the age of a horse-chestnut branch.

PUSSY WILLOW

"How do you do?" said Pussy Willow, one morning.

"I have just put on my soft gray coat.

"I have come to tell you the news: —

"Spring will soon be here!

"The other buds will be out later.

"They are waiting for Mr. Sun.

"But I do not need to wait for him to wake me up.

"My coat keeps me warm.

"My sisters are still asleep upon this very branch.

"They are little green leaf buds.

"Before they come out, a strange thing will happen to me.

"I shall be covered with tiny yellow flowers, like this: —

" Or with green flowers, like this : —

" The yellow flowers come on some willow
trees.

" These are the father trees.

" Other willows have the green flowers.

" These are the mother trees.

" Wait and see from which tree I came."

Over in the meadow,
  Where the clear pools shine,
Lived a green mother frog
  And her froggies nine.
" Croak," said the mother,
  " We croak," said the nine.
So they croaked and they splashed
  Where the clear pools shine.

—OLIVE A. WADSWORTH.

THE DANCE OF THE MAPLE KEYS

**maple keys   lawn   delight
blanket   grove**

Why, what are these?
They are a party of happy maple keys.

See them dancing with glee on a snowy lawn.
They are standing on their heads with delight.
What has made them so happy, do you say?
Just what makes us happy to-day.
Spring is coming, coming, coming.
The sun is taking off winter's snow blanket.
He has told the good news to the birds and
the seeds and the roots.
And they are all coming in answer to his call.

But what are the maple keys thinking about?

Perhaps about the beautiful grove they hope to become.

Perhaps about the tree mother that they have left.

Perhaps about the southwest wind and the warm rain.

For these will help them to grow.

And perhaps they are just happy, without thinking about it at all.

STORY OF THE MAPLE KEYS

**Norway   coral
crimson   reef**

This is the Norway maple.

It has the most beautiful bud of all the maples.

All the tiny leaves are covered with larger scales.

These scales are pale green with fine stripes of bronze.

The flowers, too, are very handsome.
But they are pale in color.

It is the red maple which has flowers like coral.

"The maples crimson to a coral reef," said Mr. Lowell.

After a time the flowers of all maples turn to fruit.

This ⌐ is a maple fruit.

And inside are the two twin maple babies.

Many times I have seen the twins swinging in the tree.

" Dear mother tree, let us go.

" We want to try our wings.

" We wish to be trees ourselves."

But the mother tree would not let them go.

" Not yet," she said.

" Wait until you are older and stronger.

" Wait until I have given you plenty of food.

" Then, when you are quite ready, I will let you go."

THE MAPLE FRUITS AGAIN

journeys   separated   discouraged

At last the mother tree had done all that she could.

The twins were full grown.

Their seed leaves were thick with food.

The babies were well covered up in their little cradles.

One day the west wind carried off some of the twins.

" Now," they said, " we can begin to be trees."

" Sun and rain, help us to grow ! " they cried.

But the sun only smiled.

And the rain wept.

They said, " Not yet, not yet, little twins ! "
Sometimes the wind carried them on short
journeys.

After a while it grew colder.
Then came snow and ice.
The twins had long since separated.
Now each was frozen to the ground.
They could not move.
The wind broke off bits of their wings.
They began to look old and brown.
They felt very much discouraged.
" Shall we ever be trees ? " they said.

*   *   *   *   *   *   *

At last spring came.
And then the maple keys had their party.
No wonder they were gay and happy.
For each maple baby had sent a little white
foot into the ground.
You call this foot a root.
But it is a foot for the little maple baby.
It helps her to stand up.
But I will tell you something very strange : —
Maple babies have mouths in their feet.
They cannot run around to get their food.
But their feet can travel.

So they have mouths in their feet.

And their feet are in the ground.

For this is where their food is.

A little later two long leaves came out of the cradle.

But they did not look like maple leaves.

The baby did not care.

He was only too glad to have any leaves.

Before long two more leaves came out of the bud.

These were just like the leaves on the mother tree.

APRIL

"Now the noisy winds are still,
April's coming up the hill."
— Mrs. Mary Mapes Dodge.

"Sweet April wakes."
— Tennyson.

THE BIRCH TREE

Hiawatha   **birch**   **canoe**   **wrapper**   **rustled**
       breeze   **patience**

Said Hiawatha : —
    " Give me of your bark, O Birch Tree
    Of your yellow bark, O Birch Tree.
    I a light canoe will build me,
    That shall float upon the river
       Like a yellow leaf in Autumn,
       Like a yellow water lily !

187

" Lay aside your cloak, O Birch Tree,
Lay aside your white skin wrapper,
For the summer time is coming,
And the sun is warm in heaven,
    And you need no white skin wrapper."

And the tree with all its branches
Rustled in the breeze of morning,
Saying, with a sigh of patience,
"Take my cloak, O Hiawatha."

THE BIRCH

especially   graceful   delicate

The birch is a beautiful tree.

The white birch is especially graceful and delicate.

It has been said of it: —

"Most beautiful of forest trees,
The Lady of the Wood."

But the canoe birch is the best known and most useful of all the birches.

It will give you a tent, or a roof, or a boat.

When it rains you may use its bark for an umbrella.

It will give you plates, spoons, letter paper, candles, and wood.

The nicest cup in the world is a birch bark cup.

It just fits the mouth.

It makes the water taste sweet.

I am thirsty now as I think of it.

And the thought of its cousin makes me hungry.

Do you know the black birch?

It may not be as beautiful as the white birch.

But it tastes so good.

Only young wintergreen leaves are more spicy.

Only the wild strawberry is more delicious.

FERN SONG

Dance to the beat of the rain, little Fern,
  And spread out your palms again,
And say, "Though the Sun
Hath my vesture spun,
  He had labored, alas! in vain,
But for the shade
That the cloud hath made,
  And the gift of the Dew and Rain."

Then laugh and upturn
All your fronds, little Fern,
  And rejoice in the beat of the rain.

—John B. Tabb.

THE POPLARS

catkins   necklace   downy

Do you remember these buds?

From some of them came red caterpillars.

No: not caterpillars. We
must say catkins.

Or we may call them poplar
flowers.

But they look like caterpillars.

After the catkins had fallen to the
ground the leaves came. Here they are: —

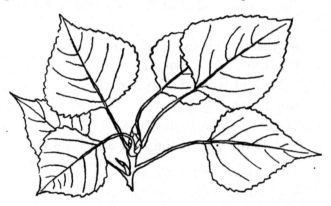

This is one of the commonest of city trees.
It grows very rapidly even in the city.

But the leaves fall soon.

Sometimes it is called the Necklace Poplar.

This is because of its catkins.

But most people call it the North Carolina Poplar.

Here are the leaves of one of its cousins : —

They are white and downy on the under side.

So it is called the white Poplar.

Sometimes the wind blows the white sides uppermost.

Then some people say : —

" It will rain soon."

And so it often does.

THE WALNUT TREE THAT WANTED TO BEAR TULIPS.

grower   different   velvety   greet
stranger   sawed

Once upon a time a young Walnut lived in the back yard of a tulip grower.

The Walnut tree loved the tulips.

He was glad that the sun was good to them.

Still he did wish that the sun would pay him a long visit, too.

The tree knew every tulip in the garden.

He said good-morning to them each day.

And he gave each new one a hearty welcome.

One day a strange tulip bloomed.

o

It was different from all of the others.

Its color was a deep velvety black.

When the Walnut tree saw this tulip, he danced for joy.

His branches bent down to greet the wonderful stranger.

His leaves kissed her.

More than ever he wished that he could bear tulips.

He went to work with a will.

He sent his roots deep into the big garden.

He spread his branches to get all the sunlight.

And this he did bravely for over a hundred years.

The Walnut tree was beautiful to look upon.

But it had never borne tulips.

One day a wood carver went by.

"This is a perfect tree," he said.

"It is just what I need for my work."

So the tree was cut down.

Its wood was sawn and cut.

But the Walnut did not care.

For what do you think the wood carver was making?

BEAUTIFUL BLACK TULIPS!

THE ELM

**famous   General   Washington   command
American   William Penn   Indian
friendly**

I am a famous tree.
Under me once stood
the   great   General
Washington.

It was the day before
the Fourth of July.

But there was no
Fourth of July then.

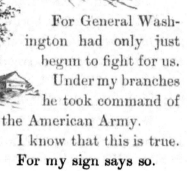

For General Wash-
ington had only just
begun to fight for us.

Under my branches
he took command of
the American Army.

I know that this is true.
For my sign says so.

Here is a friend of mine.
He is no longer living.

But once upon a time a great man stood under his branches.

The name of the great man was William Penn.

He met the Indians here.

They were always friendly to him after this.

For they knew that he was fair.

Now you know how beautiful I am.

These are my flowers.

After the flowers come beautiful fruits.

And later still come these leaves.

WHO AM I?

hyacinth   nosegay

Do you know my name?

I am a large tree with very beautiful white flowers.

The bees love me.

For I give them honey.

Children love me because I am beautiful.

Sometimes they call me a Hyacinth tree.

For my flowers do look like a hyacinth.

Then again, they pretend that I am the nosegay of a giant.

I think that I look something like a Christmas tree.

My flowers are the candles.

Here is my fruit.

And here is my large seed.
It looks something like a chestnut.
Now I am sure that you know my name.

Yes : that is right.

I am the Horse-chestnut tree.

I am the Linden.
Do you not think my flowers beautiful?
So do the bees !

You must
know my name.
My branches
are so gnarled.
Even in win-
ter you can tell
who I am.
But I am
most beautiful
in my summer
dress.

TO VIOLETS

**welcome   maids-of-honor   respected
neglected**

Welcome, maids of honor!
You do bring
In the Spring
And wait upon her.

She has maidens many,
   Fresh and fair;
      Yet you are
   More sweet than any.

Yet though thus respected,
      By and bye
         You do lie
   Poor girls! neglected.

—ROBERT HERRICK.

NARCISSUS

Narcissus   hunting   companions   fountain

Narcissus had been hunting in the forest all day.

He had lost his companions.

While looking for them, he saw a fountain.

He knelt down on the bank to drink.

He saw a beautiful face in the water.

He thought that it was the sprite of the fountain.

"You are the most beautiful woman that I have ever seen," he said.

"Come to me, and I will always love you."

The face smiled back at him.

But she said nothing.

Day after day Narcissus hung over the fountain.

He forgot to eat and drink.

He did not even sleep.

And at last he died of grief.

For he never knew that it was his own beautiful face in the fountain.

His friends came to carry away his body.

They could not find it.

But from the edge of the water a flower rose.

And for him they named it the Narcissus.

LITTLE ANEMONE

anemone   messenger   swayed   petaled

Little anemone,
  So frail and fair,
Blooming so brave
  In the cold spring
      air.

Sweet little messen-
      ger,
  Sent here to tell,
Summer is coming
  And all will be well.

Standing so firm,
  Though swayed by the breeze,
Seeming to say
  By its pure petaled leaves:

Out of the darkness
  Shall come forth light,
God in His wisdom
  Has made day and night.

—H. S. Pike, *from Fairy Land of Flowers.*

SPRING FLOWERS

early   Hepatica   purple   Dogtooth Violet

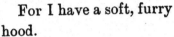

We are the early flowers.
Can you call us all by name?
My name is Hepatica.
Just as soon as I hear the robin
I put my head above the ground.
I can come earlier than most
flowers.

For I have a soft, furry
hood.

But it soon gets too
warm for me.

So I throw it off.

My gown is lavender.

But my sisters wear
different colors.

Some are dressed in
purple.

Others wear pink, or
even white.

*   *   *   *   *

My name is Spring Beauty.

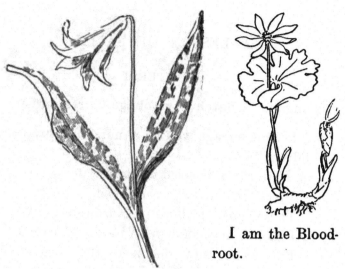

I am the Blood-
root.

And I am a stately yellow lily.
Trout lily some call me.
This is because I have speckled leaves.
But most people call me Dogtooth Violet.
I have not the least idea why they do this.

A LESSON OF FAITH

CHAPTER I

engage   hatch   cabbage   remember

" Let me engage you as a nurse for my poor children."

A Butterfly was speaking to a Caterpillar.

" I feel very ill," she continued.

" These eggs which you see are mine.

" I do not know how soon they will hatch.

" But when they do, feed them on early dew.

" Get them honey from the flowers.

" Do not let them fly about too much at first.

" What a pity it is that you cannot fly yourself.

" But I have no time to look for another nurse.

" Dear! why did I lay my eggs on a cabbage leaf ?

" But you will be kind to my poor little ones.

" How dizzy I am !

" Remember the food, Caterpillar."

With these words, the Butterfly died.

. The poor Caterpillar had no chance to say either yes or no.

But there were the eggs right before her.

" A pretty nurse she has chosen, poor lady.

" They will not mind me when they feel the gay wings on their back."

But the Caterpillar had a kind heart.

She made up her mind to do her best.

CHAPTER II

believe   easily

" Two heads are better than one," said the Caterpillar.

" I will ask some wise animal about the matter."

Still she did not know whom to ask.

There was the dog, — but then he was so rough.

And the cat who came to the garden cared for nothing but herself.

At last she thought of the Lark.

The Lark listened to her story.

Then he went singing into the blue sky.

The Caterpillar could not hear a sound.

At last the Lark began to be heard again.

The Caterpillar almost jumped for joy.

" News, news, brother Caterpillar," sung the Lark.

" But the worst of it is, you will not believe me."

"I believe everything I am told," said the Caterpillar.

" Well, then, I will tell you what these little caterpillars are to eat."

" Dew and honey from the flowers," said the Caterpillar.

" Nothing of the kind," said the Lark.

" They are to eat something that you can easily get for them."

" But I can get nothing easily except cabbage leaves," said the Caterpillar.

" Good," said the Lark.

" You are to feed them on cabbage leaves ! "

" Never," said the Caterpillar.

" But why do you ask me, and then not believe me ?

" You have no faith."

" Oh, I believe everything I am told," said the Caterpillar.

" No, you do not.

" You do not even believe about the food.

" Now tell me what you think the eggs will become."

" Butterflies, of course."

" Caterpillars," said the Lark.

" You will find it all out in time," he added, as he flew away.

CHAPTER III

foolish   cruel

" I thought that the Lark was wise," said the Caterpillar.

" But he is foolish and unkind.

" But what does he see when he flies so high?"

" I would tell you if you would believe me," said the Lark.

" I believe everything I am told," said the Caterpillar.

" Then I will tell you something. Some day you will be a butterfly yourself!"

" Go away! You are cruel and foolish."

" But I said that you would not believe me," said the Lark.

Just then the Caterpillar felt something moving.

There were eight or ten tiny caterpillars.

They were already eating the cabbage.

They had broken from the Butterfly's eggs.

At first the Caterpillar was very much ashamed.

Then she was glad.

For she thought that perhaps she, too, would be a butterfly after all.

———◆———

LITTLE WHITE LILY

droopeth   drooping

Little White Lily
Sat by a stone,
Drooping and waiting
Till the sun shone.

Little White Lily
Sunshine has fed.
Little White Lily
Is lifting her head.

Little White Lily
Droopeth with pain,
Waiting and waiting
For the wet rain.

P

Little White Lily
Holdeth her cup;
Rain is fast falling
And filling it up.

Little White Lily
Smells very sweet.
On her head sunshine,
Rain at her feet.

Thanks to the sunshine,
Thanks to the rain,
Little White Lily
Is happy again.

—GEORGE MACDONALD

Indians   settlers   clearing
disappear   misfortune

Once there were no white people in America.
Only Indians lived here.
There were no cities and towns then.
The whole land was covered with forests.
The first thing that the white settlers did
was to cut down some trees.
They called this making a "clearing."
Out of the trees they built their log-cabins.
At last the forest began to disappear.
This was a misfortune.

For the living trees are very good to us.

They give us shade.

They give us better air.

They bring the rain.

They break the force of the storms.

Still we must have the dead trees too.

We need them for lumber, for fuel, and for manufacturing.

What can we do about it?

We can plant new trees.

Our wise country knows this.

So she asks us to join her in planting trees on Arbor Day.

MAY

" In May the valley lilies ring,
    Their bells chime clear and sweet,
They cry, ' Come forth, ye flowerets all
    And dance with twinkling feet.' "
                   — *From the German.*

MAY

Pretty little violets,
  Waking from your sleep;
Fragrant little blossoms,
  Just about to peep.
Would you know the reason
  All the world is gay?
Listen to the bobolink
  Telling you 'tis May!

Little ferns and grasses,
   All so green and bright,
Purple clover nodding,
   Daisies fresh and white.
Would you know the reason
   All the world is gay?
Listen to the bobolink
   Telling you 'tis May!

Darling little warblers,
   Coming in the spring,
Would you know the reason
   That you love to sing?
Hear the merry children
   Shouting as they play,
Listen to the bobolink
   Telling us 'tis May! [1]

[1] From *Songs and Games for Little Ones*, by Walker and Jenks. Reprinted by permission of the Oliver Ditson Company, owners of the copyright.

THE SWALLOW

sowing   flax   linen
discovered   begged

A swallow saw a man sowing seeds in the ground.

She went behind him and picked up one of the seeds.

She found that it was flax.

"Soon this flax will be grain," she said.

"Then it will be made into linen thread.

"Then perhaps it will be made into nets to catch us birds."

So she went to all the birds.

She told them what she had discovered.

She begged them to come to help her eat up the flax seed.

But the birds would not listen to her.

Not one of them would help her.

The young flax began to grow.

The Swallow again tried to get the birds to help her.

But they only made fun of her.

And the flax kept on growing.

The Swallow saw how careless the birds were.

So she left the woods.

She came to live among men.

She built her nests in barns and along the eaves of houses.

Has a wise little swallow never looked at you with bright eyes?

Do you know what she tried to say to you?

It was this: —

Dear child, do not wait until it is too late to do what ought to be done now.

— Adapted from ÆSOP.

THE CONCEITED APPLE BRANCH

princess   noticed   fault

It was the month of May.

The wind still blew cold.

But from bush and tree, field and flower, came the sound : —

" Spring has come."

A young princess was driving slowly by.

She saw a beautiful branch of apple blossoms.

She carried them home with her to the castle.

Nearly every one said something about the branch.

And the apple branch soon learned that there were many different people in the world.

He looked out of the open window.

He saw too that even the plants were rich and poor, ugly and beautiful.

He noticed a little common yellow flower that grew everywhere.

It even grew between paving stones and in the city.

" Poor little plants," said the apple blossom.

" It is not your fault that you are ugly.

"It is not your fault that you have the ugly name of dandelion.

"No; but it is with plants as with men.

"There must be a difference."

"A difference," cried the sunbeam.

He kissed the apple blossom as he spoke.

And then he kissed the yellow dandelion in the field.

The sunbeam knew better.

wreaths   picked   breath   whoever

A number of children came across the field.

The youngest laughed when he saw the dandelions.

He kissed them with delight.

The older children made wreaths and chains and belts of them.

They picked carefully some of those that had gone to seed.

Then some tried to blow them all off with one breath.

For they knew that whoever did so would have new clothes soon.

"Do you see," said the sunbeam, "the beauty of the dandelions?"

"Yes, to children they are beautiful," said the apple blossom.

**blunt   conceited   feathery   strong
blushed**

By and by an old woman came into the field.

In her hand she carried a blunt knife.

She dug out the roots of the dandelion with it.

With some of them she made tea for herself.

But others she sold.

With the money she bought milk and sugar.

"But beauty is better than all this," said the conceited apple blossoms.

Just then the princess came into the room.

In her hand she carried something that seemed like a flower.

She covered it carefully from the wind.

What do you think it was?

It was the feathery seed crown of a dandelion!

"See," she said, "how beautiful it is!

"I will paint it in a picture with the apple blossoms."

Then the sunbeam kissed again the dandelion and the apple blossoms.

And the apple blossom blushed.

— *Adapted from* ANDERSEN.

THE DANDELION

With locks of gold to-day;
To-morrow, silver gray;
Then blossom bald. Behold,
O man! thy fortune told.

—JOHN B. TABB.

———◆———

A STORY OF THE DANDELION

usually   naughty   reached   lonely
rubbed

Once upon a time a great many little stars
lived in the sky.

Their father was the Sun.

The Moon was their mother.

Usually they were very good little children.

They liked to brighten the sky.

But one night their mother called to them to
come to their work.

They came very slowly.

They did not shine when she told them to do
so.

What do you think old Mother Moon did ?

She called up from the earth some good little stars.

They were only flowers on earth.

But they did the very best that they could.

So they were changed into stars in the sky.

The naughty stars felt themselves falling — falling — falling.

At last they reached the earth.

They cried, and cried, and cried.

For they were lonely, and very sorry for what they had done.

At last they fell asleep.

In the morning the Sun came.

He shone so brightly that everything woke.

Even his little children, the stars, rubbed open their eyes.

Then they began to cry again.

For they remembered how naughty they had been.

Their father, the Sun, felt sorry for them.

So he told them they might shine on the earth.

So now the stars shine in heaven at night.

And the dandelions shine in the grass during the day.

THE DANDELION

**rosette   upwards   divide   enough
plenty**

Every one knows   me.
My name is dande-   lion.
And I am, indeed, a   dandy lion.
For there is no place   so poor that I can-
not live in it.
And then I make it   beautiful.
Have you ever seen   me growing in
a sandy place?

I look like this.

My leaves make a little rosette.

But in the grass I am quite different.

Then my leaves reach upwards.

If I did not make a rosette of myself in the sand what would happen ?

Why, other plants would try to grow in the same place.

We would have to divide the food.

There would not be enough for any of us.

And perhaps we would all die.

But suppose that I should make a rosette of myself in the grass ?

Then it would be very bad for the grass.

I should shade it so that it could not grow.

Q

Or else it would be very bad for me.

For the Sun could not find me if the grass did grow.

And we plants must have plenty of light.

Here I am again!

Once I was yellow.

My stem was short.

I shone like a star in the green grass.

The bees came to visit me on sunny days.

On rainy days and at night I slept.

This was to keep the honey nice for the bees

One day the Sun called me, as usual.

But I did not wake up.

I hid my head.

For I was no longer beautiful.

But look at me now.

My stem is long.

I was never so tall before.

Look at my head.

It is covered with lovely white hair.

It must be that I am an old man.

These white hairs must be seeds.

Look at them.

Are they not like balloons?

Some day West Wind will call them.

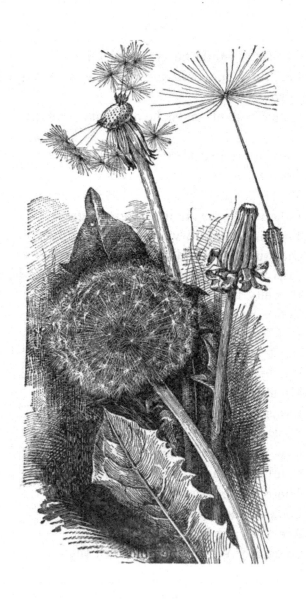

They will fly away with him.

Then I shall be, indeed, an old, old man.

For I shall be bald.

But I am glad of it.

For each of my seeds may grow into another whole plant.

And little children love us so.

———◆———

ANOTHER STORY OF THE DANDELION

South Wind is fat and lazy.

He lives where it is always summer.

Sometimes he brings to us things from this summer land.

In the spring he sends the robins and blue-birds.

Then he brings the swallows and the wild geese.

Without him the melons and grapes would not grow.

One day he was looking toward us, northward.

Then he saw a beautiful maiden.

Her garments were brightest green.

Her hair had in it the gold of the sunshine.

South Wind loved her.

Every day he looked upon her.

But he was too fat and lazy to go to her.

So he only sighed and looked.

One morning her beautiful yellow hair was white.

It looked as if it were covered with snow-flakes.

"North Wind," he said.

"You have stolen the maiden from me.

"I saw the touch of your hand on her head."

He sighed, and sighed again.

Then the air seemed full of snowflakes.

The maiden with hair like sunshine was gone forever.

Poor, poor South Wind!

It was no woman that you looked at.

It was no maiden that you sighed for.

It was the dandelion!

— Adapted from Hiawatha.

THE TAX-GATHERER

surprise   eye-glass   publican
collecting   tax

"And pray, who are you?"
  Said the violet blue
To the bee, with surprise
  At his wonderful size,
In her eye-glass of dew.

"I, madam," said he,
  "Am a publican bee
Collecting the tax
  On honey and wax.
Have you nothing for me?"
                    —JOHN B. TABB.

STORY OF THE APPLE BLOSSOM

**stirring   decided   orchard   delicious
handkerchiefs**

It was a bright sunny May morning.
The worker bees were up and stirring.
They were out on a honey hunt.

But they had not yet decided which flower
to visit.
They went by an old orchard.
The bees stopped a moment.
Certainly there was an odor of delicious
honey in the air.

Then all at once little pink and white handkerchiefs began to flutter in the wind.

And they heard the voices of the apple
blossoms saying: —

"This way, little bees.

"Walk right in and help yourselves.

"Our finest honey is at your service."

And the bees did walk right in.

They helped themselves to all that they could
find.

Then out they walked again.

Not one said anything about paying for the
honey either.

But they did pay for it, too.

For they carried the flower dust from flower
to flower.

The yellow flower dust helps the seeds to
grow.

Wise little apple blossoms!

Now I know why you smell so sweet.

Now I know why you are so beautiful.

It is not for me.

It is for the bees.

And it is not for the bees either.

It is for your seed babies.

But I love you just the same.

And is this the Apple Blossom?

It certainly is.

But where are her five pretty pink and white handkerchiefs?

You must look for them on the ground now.

The Apple Blossom called the bees with them.

The bees came.

They carried her flower dust around for her.

Now she wants to give everything to her little seed babies.

So she drops the five little handkerchiefs to the ground.

All the juice goes to the babies and the babies' home.

* * * * * * *

And here is the Apple Blossom again.

See how thick she has grown.

She is a little green apple now.

All summer long she will grow thicker and thicker.

But you will have to look sharp to see her.

For she is the color of the green leaves.

"A rose is a rose when it blooms,
An apple is a rose when it ripens."

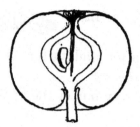

Look at the apples now.

How beautiful they are.

What boy could help eating them?

But this will end all the poor Apple Blossom's work.

No, indeed.

It is just what she wants us to do.

For then she can be sure that her seed babies will be planted somewhere.

Look at the cut apples.

Do you see a green line?

Most of the apple is between it and the skin.

This was once the little green flower cup inside.

And in the eye were once the five little handkerchiefs.

This is where the little moth lays her egg.

She does this when the apple is very small.

The egg hatches into a little caterpillar.

This caterpillar gets fatter and fatter as the apple grows larger.

Then at last it eats its way out of the apple.

TWO COMMON WEEDS

Shepherd's Purse   precious
Sheep's Sorrel   buck-
wheat   cousin

" You may not know our names.

" But you must have seen us many times.

" For both of us grow even along city streets."

" My name is Shepherd's Purse," says one.

"And a very good name it is.

" Open my purses.

" You will find something more precious than gold.

" They are my little seed babies.

"Some day they too will grow into beautiful plants with white flowers."

Then the other little plant spoke out.

" I am sure I do not know why I am called Sheep's Sorrel.

" But that is my name.

" I am not very much use in the world.

" Still many people like to look at me.

" Perhaps you did not know it.

" But it is my tiny flowers and fruit that make the meadows so red.

" My relatives are useful.

" Without my near cousin you would not have had buckwheat cakes this winter.

" So love me for my cousin's sake.

" And love me for myself too."

" ' The Dogwood pitches his broad white tent
on the edge of the woods.' "

JACK–IN–THE–PULPIT

Jack-in-the-Pulpit   preaches   surplice
sermon   text   expound   discuss

Jack-in-the-Pulpit
Preaches to-day,
Under the green trees
Just over the way.

Green is his surplice,
Green are his bands;
In his queer little pulpit
The little priest stands.

So much for the preacher —
The sermon comes next.
Shall we tell how he preached it,
And where was his text?

We heard not the preacher
Expound or discuss;
But we looked at the people
And they looked at us.

We heard the wind organ,
The bee and the bird —
But of Jack-in-the-Pulpit
We heard not a word.

— *Adapted from* Whittier's *Child Life.* — CLARA SMITH.

"Buttercups' faces
    Beaming and bright,
Clovers with bonnets,
    Some red and some white."

THE LILAC

· lavender   daintiest   tinted   syrup
caramel

The sun shone warm, and the lilac said,
" I must hurry and get my table spread,
For if I am slow, and dinner late,
My friends, the bees, will have to wait."

So delicate lavender glass she brought
And the daintiest china ever bought,
Purple tinted, and all complete;
And she filled each cup with honey sweet.

" Dinner is ready!" the spring wind cried;
And from hive and hiding far and wide,
While the lilac laughed to see them come,
The little gray-jacketed bees came hum-m!

They sipped the syrup from every cell,
They nibbled at taffy and caramel;
Then, without being asked, they all buzzed, "We
Will be very happy to stay to tea."

— CLARA DOTY BATES.

AMERICA

My country, 'tis of thee,
Sweet land of liberty,
    Of thee I sing;
Land where my fathers died,
Land of the Pilgrims' pride,
From every mountain side
    Let freedom ring.

Our fathers' God to thee,
Author of Liberty,
    To thee we sing.
Long may our land be bright
With freedom's holy light;
Protect us by thy might,
    Great God, our King.

DECORATION DAY

**bouquet   trimmed   cemetery   buried
Civil War**

What a joy it is to watch the coming of spring.

A faint green color creeps over the brown fields.

The buds on the trees begin to swell.

One morning there are tender green leaves.

In May the flowers come.

One day in May the teacher says : —

"Children, bring some flowers for Decoration Day."

Next morning in walks a huge bouquet.

The teacher sees a pair of little feet below it

She hears a voice say : —

"If you please, this is for Decoration Day."

In the streets everybody is carrying flowers.

The houses are trimmed with flags.

Bands of music are playing.

Soldiers are marching.

Where is everybody going ?

They are going to the cemetery.

Flags flutter over many graves.

There brave soldiers lie buried.

And there the people will scatter the flowers.

These are the soldiers who died in our civil war.

They are " boys in blue."

And they are the " boys in gray."

Every year we give one day to thinking of them.

And this day is Decoration Day.

JUNE

"June! dear June!
Now God be praised for June."

— Lowell.

THE JUMPERS

flea   polite   graceful

The Flea, the Grasshopper, and the Frog
wanted to see who could jump the highest.

The Whale came to see them jump.

" I will give my daughter to the best jumper,"
said the king.

The Flea came first.

He bowed politely to everybody.

But then, you see, he has always lived with people.

No wonder he was polite and knew what to do.

Next came the Grasshopper.

He was not so graceful as the Flea.

But he wore beautiful green clothes.

He said that he could sing very well.

Both the Flea and the Grasshopper talked much about themselves.

The Frog said nothing.

The Flea jumped very high.

No one could see what had become of him.

The Grasshopper only jumped half as high.

He jumped in the king's face.

The king thought him very rude.

The Frog stood for a long time thinking.

" I am afraid he is ill," said the dog.

But suddenly he made a jump into the lap of the princess.

" There is nothing higher than my daughter," said the king.

" The Frog has made the highest jump that can be made.

"He has shown that he has sense."

And so he won the princess.

— *Adapted from* ANDERSEN.

THE DONKEY AND THE GRASSHOPPER

donkey   chirp

A Donkey heard the grasshoppers chirp one day.

He was much pleased with the sound.

He wished that he could make such sweet music.

"What sort of food do you eat?" he said to the grasshoppers.

"Your voices are so very charming."

The grasshoppers replied : —

"We live upon dew."

Of course this was not true.

But the Donkey decided that he, too, would live on dew.

And in a short time he died from hunger!

— Adapted from Æsop.

THE BLUEBELL

valley   mountains   enjoyed   remembered

This is the bluebell.
Have you ever seen it growing?
It chooses bits of rock for a home.
Listen, and I will tell you its story: —
Once upon a time there lived a little white flower.
It grew in a deep valley.
On every side were the mountains.
And on the mountains grew the trees.
This made the valley very dark.
But there was a little strip of blue sky.
It was just above the flower's head.
Every day it would look up.

It would say to itself: —

"What a beautiful blue sky!"

But at night it loved the sky even more.

For a bright star came and smiled at the flower.

All day long the flower enjoyed the blue sky.

All day long she thought of the bright star.

Then, when night came, she remembered the blue sky.

And she was happy in the light of the star.

Then a strange thing happened.

The little flower turned blue as the sky.

And one morning it found in its blue cup a drop of dew.

And the dewdrop shone like the star!

Little children, too, grow to be like what they love.

"Pray, where have the charming bluebells gone,
  That lately bloomed in the wood?
Why, the little fairies have each taken one,
  And put it on for a hood."

— Little Flower Folks.

FOR FLAG DAY

spangled   lawyer   British   Baltimore
             rockets   famous

" 'Tis the star spangled banner !
Oh, long may it wave
While the land of the free
Is the home of the brave ! "

Everybody knows this beautiful song.

And everybody should know the story of the man who wrote it.

Francis Scott Key was a young American lawyer.   He wanted to visit a friend.

This friend was a prisoner on board a British vessel.

Key went to the ship carrying a white flag.

Trieste

Trieste Publishing has a massive catalogue of classic book titles. Our aim is to provide readers with the highest quality reproductions of fiction and non-fiction literature that has stood the test of time. The many thousands of books in our collection have been sourced from libraries and private collections around the world.

The titles that Trieste Publishing has chosen to be part of the collection have been scanned to simulate the original. Our readers see the books the same way that their first readers did decades or a hundred or more years ago. Books from that period are often spoiled by imperfections that did not exist in the original. Imperfections could be in the form of blurred text, photographs, or missing pages. It is highly unlikely that this would occur with one of our books. Our extensive quality control ensures that the readers of Trieste Publishing's books will be delighted with their purchase. Our staff has thoroughly reviewed every page of all the books in the collection, repairing, or if necessary, rejecting titles that are not of the highest quality. This process ensures that the reader of one of Trieste Publishing's titles receives a volume that faithfully reproduces the original, and to the maximum degree possible, gives them the experience of owning the original work.

We pride ourselves on not only creating a pathway to an extensive reservoir of books of the finest quality, but also providing value to every one of our readers. Generally, Trieste books are purchased singly - on demand, however they may also be purchased in bulk. Readers interested in bulk purchases are invited to contact us directly to enquire about our tailored bulk rates. Email: customerservice@triestepublishing.com

You May Also Like

ISBN: 9780649655618
Paperback: 212 pages
Dimensions: 6.14 x 0.45 x 9.21 inches
Language: eng

Nature Study in Elementary Schools: Second Reader. Myths, Stories, Poems

Lucy Langdon Williams Wilson

ISBN: 9780649655601
Paperback: 284 pages
Dimensions: 6.14 x 0.60 x 9.21 inches
Language: eng

Nature Study in Elementary Schools: First Reader

Lucy Langdon Williams Wilson

www.triestepublishing.com

You May Also Like

Nature study in elementary schools; first reader

Lucy Langdon Williams Wilson

ISBN: 9780649211050
Paperback: 280 pages
Dimensions: 6.14 x 0.59 x 9.21 inches
Language: eng

Nature study in elementary schools; second reader, myths, stories, poems

Mrs. Lucy Langdon Williams Wilson

ISBN: 9780649162154
Paperback: 216 pages
Dimensions: 6.14 x 0.46 x 9.21 inches
Language: eng

www.triestepublishing.com

You May Also Like

1807-1907 The One Hundredth Anniversary of the incorporation of the Town of Arlington Massachusetts

Various

ISBN: 9780649420544
Paperback: 108 pages
Dimensions: 6.14 x 0.22 x 9.21 inches
Language: eng

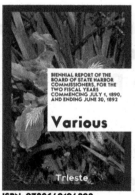

Biennial report of the Board of State Harbor Commissioners, for the two fiscal years commencing July 1, 1890, and ending June 30, 1892

Various

ISBN: 9780649194292
Paperback: 44 pages
Dimensions: 6.14 x 0.09 x 9.21 inches
Language: eng

You May Also Like

Biennial report of the Board of State Harbor Commissioners for the two fisca years. Commeneing July 1, 1884, and Ending June 30, 1886

Various

ISBN: 9780649199693
Paperback: 48 pages
Dimensions: 6.14 x 0.10 x 9.21 inches
Language: eng

Biennial report of the Board of state commissioners, for the two fiscal years, commencing July 1, 1890, and ending June 30, 1892

Various

ISBN: 9780649196395
Paperback: 44 pages
Dimensions: 6.14 x 0.09 x 9.21 inches
Language: eng

Find more of our titles on our website. We have a selection of thousands of titles that will interest you. Please visit

www.triestepublishing.com